Tom
Wishing you much
for your 30th bir
All our Love
Mum & Dad
xxx

THE BUSINESS OF
PERSONAL TRAINING

THE BUSINESS OF PERSONAL TRAINING

Marketing Strategies for the Profitable Personal Trainer

ANDREA OH

PHOENIX
Interactive Consulting
Chicago, IL MMXVI

DEDICATION

For the risk-takers and innovators who relentlessly
follow their dreams, despite the doubters and naysayers
who fear the impossible.

TABLE OF CONTENTS

LIST OF FIGURES

FOREWORD

I'm not a writer. I've never had the ability to bring the written word to the masses in a way that truly entertains, informs and inspires. It's a gift, and a gift that, when combined with a passion for the message, allows the reader to be transformed. It leaves the reader a little bit smarter or, at the very least, makes them use their brain for their own betterment.

I am, on the other hand, passionate about the fitness industry. After 30 years in the industry, I continue to do what I can to lead and inspire others with the projects I involve myself with, including the tight-knit communities I get to cultivate that support these efforts. I have been fortunate to know Andrea for over fifteen of these years and have had the pleasure of working with her on a handful of these projects.

Andrea is also incredibly passionate about the fitness industry. She has dedicated over two decades of her life to innovating and educating the industry she loves. And, unlike me, she IS A WRITER.

Read through the pages of "The Business of Personal Training: Marketing Strategies for the Profitable Personal Trainer" and her passion for the marketing process is clear and compelling. It's one thing to know the subject matter, but it's quite another to bring it to life! Perhaps it's the combination of her personal experience, education and upbringing, but it's certainly not easy and continues to impress me.

After three decades in the health and fitness industry, one of the biggest lessons I've learned is that marketing matters ... more than most care to believe. It is, without a doubt, the most important investment you can make in your brand. This is where I refer to "BIG M" and "little M".

"WHAT?", you ask?

"Big marketing (BIG M)" refers to the overall brand and the power of brand messaging, essence, creative and the "red thread" of how one's brand is portrayed. BIG M fuels the brand's expectations. It is your company's "Why":
- Why should I buy from you?
- Do we believe in the same things?
- Do we have the same core values?
- Will you deliver on the services you promise to deliver?

This is what the BIG M helps you communicate. Little marketing (little M)" transforms that message into the advertising and outward "voice" of your brand. It gets the BIG M message out there in various mediums.

"The Business of Personal Training: Marketing Strategies for the Profitable Personal Trainer" is a methodical and clearly articulated road map to setting up a comprehensive marketing plan for your business. This step-by-step guide takes you through everything you need to know about the importance, strategy, tactics and execution of a marketing game plan that fits your personal training business. It helps you articulate your BIG M and understand the best tools for your little M.

Never before have there been as many options to drive your message directly to your targeted customer. Thankfully, Andrea's book teaches you how to make smart choices that fit your brand, budget and business objectives.

There is a great divide that small business owners have to struggle with on a daily basis ... whether to work "IN" the business or "ON" the business. More experienced business people understand they have to cross this divide frequently and with purpose. Unfortunately, most fitness entrepreneurs are NOT experienced business people.

Naturally, the "technician" in you wants to do what you love. This could include providing actual training services, meeting and greeting your clients or members, or even meticulously cleaning the facility. This is what we call working "IN" your business. These tasks keep your personal training business running but do NOT grow the business.

On the other hand, the content found in the pages of this book focus readers on activities that specifically work "ON" the business. For most of us, these tasks are not easy, comfortable or even enjoyable parts of owning a business. But, because they are covered in great detail in "The Business of Personal Training: Marketing Strategies for the Profitable Personal Trainer", they are critical to your success.

Marketing, as Andrea explains in this book, is often the last thing personal trainers think about and is the first thing we cut (or think we don't need). I can tell you (from experience) that kind of thinking is a huge mistake.

I encourage you to sit back, turn off your "IN" brain and use your "ON" brain. I've never seen a book that covers the myriad of issues involved in marketing the business of personal training in a way that is so comprehensive and well written.

Andrea ... Congratulations, my friend! You continue to inspire me in everything you do and the lives you touch!

Rich Novelli
President/COO, Wellgate Sports Club
(www.wellgatesportsclub.com)

PREFACE

Growing up in a small town (in northern Canada), a career in fitness was not something that ever crossed my mind. Coming from a first generation Chinese-Canadian family, my only thought was about becoming a doctor or a surgeon. It was a sought after and stable career that involved helping people and making a difference in other people's lives.

As I got older, and sports came into the picture, I became more focused on an athletic career and the dream of professional sports. Getting a degree in exercise physiology happened by accident as the faculty of physical education was the first acceptance letter I received (I had already made the women's volleyball team and needed an acceptance letter to make it official). To appease my family I chose the most "scientific" route and focused my studies on sports sciences and the study of human movement.

I was fortunate to have celebrated many accomplishments in my athletic career but there weren't a lot options for jobs when I got back to "reality". I was fortunate to have the support of the University but essentially had to start from square one as a fitness professional.

With over four years of academic training and hands on experience working with athletes I thought I was ready to make the most of this career. Unfortunately, I was sadly mistaken.

I knew quite a bit about the human body, the science of exercise, and the psychology of motivation and focus ... but I didn't know a single thing about business or how to make money as an entrepreneur!

Being a bull-headed Taurus, I refused to let the struggles I faced each day get the best of me. I spent the next five years establishing myself as a personal trainer and strength and conditioning coach, but struggled to make ends meet. I then got an opportunity to work for a large corporation, with a decent paycheck, and I made the tough decision to leave the fitness industry for something new. Although the next three years were incredibly challenging and took me out of my comfort zone, I wouldn't change it for the world!

These years in a corporate environment ended up being my "real life" business degree. I gained hands on experience and learned about:
- Basic business knowledge
- Communications skills
- Management skills
- Business economics
- Sales and marketing

I took my new found knowledge and ventured back into the fitness industry with an optimistic outlook for the future. Again, I was naive in thinking I was prepared for ultimate success. As a result, the next ten years proved to be my "advanced" business degree in the fitness industry.

Knowing that I needed to continue to learn the business "ropes", I got my foot in the door working with a large fitness club chain as both an elite personal trainer and membership sales associate. Once I had learned as much as I could with that company, I then took a position with the world's largest Pilates organization heading up external education sales and development (while managing a small training studio out of my home ... my own fitness business "lab").

When I was ready, I left the safety of a 9 to 5 job and decided to go into business for myself as a studio owner and fitness consultant. I took on projects with a well-known corporate wellness group and started a company providing communications and technology solutions for fitness clubs. This then led to the creation of a global technology company that implemented over 100 interactive gaming clubs worldwide in less than three years.

SO WHAT?!?!?

Well ... I've done a lot of things in many areas of the fitness industry over the last fifteen years and have gained valuable knowledge no course in school could have ever taught me. Although I've faced many failures (some colossal) along the way, I have taken my learnings and now have an incredible career helping other fitness professionals and organizations around the world run their businesses more effectively and profitably.

In the end, I am still here to tell the tale and share my learnings with the world through my writing. What became evident to me early on was that fitness professionals aren't given the right tools to truly succeed in business (especially after a weekend certification course). The training is focused on exercises and programs, with no mention of how to operate a business, selling personal training, or getting the word out there with marketing. The world of business can be very cruel and entrepreneurs need to be well prepared to own a business that succeeds.

The "Business of Personal Training" series of books are written to provide fitness professionals with the business knowledge they can use to help their businesses grow. Although all aspects of business are important, this book ("Marketing Strategies for the Profitable Personal Trainer") touches on one of the most important and misunderstood concepts ... marketing.

My goal in writing this book is to provide fitness professionals with an outline of what marketing is, how important it is to building any business, and ways to effectively and efficiently apply strategies designed to increase brand awareness and ultimately grow long-term personal training sales.

I want you to avoid the costly mistakes I (and countless others) have made in the past.

I want you to have the knowledge and experience of someone who has successfully built businesses in the fitness industry from the ground up and helped others thrive.

I want you to take full advantage of the amazing business opportunities available to you through fitness.

I want you to harness the power of the Internet and all the ways it can market for you 24/7, 365 days of the year.

I want you to maintain your passion and excitement for helping others improve their lives through physical activity and exercise (while still growing your business with strategic marketing tactics).

I want you to become an inspiring success story as your own personal training business becomes the success you envision.

Andrea Oh
Founder, Business.fit *(formerly TodaysFitnessTrainer.com)*
Partner, Swank Media Inc. *(www.swankmedia.ca)*
Author, *"The Business of Personal Training: Essential Guide for the Successful Personal Trainer"* and *"GET MOTIVATED: Powerful Quotes and Exercise Tips to Inspire 52 Weeks of Extraordinary Workouts"*.

INTRODUCTION

With over two decades of experience in the fitness industry, I have come to realize the majority of fitness entrepreneurs don't understand what marketing is or what it can do to exponentially grow their business.

This is because most people are focused on selling right away to recoup money invested up front to get started. They see immediate reward for their selling efforts, even though the process of selling may not be that easy. For most, marketing is seen as unnecessary and a "nice to have" option.

On the contrary, I believe marketing is more important than sales because it gets your potential clients ready to buy ... and helps them "feel good" about opening their wallets for your fitness services.

For example, imagine you are putting your house up for sale on the market. The house is vacant and completely empty. As you take potential buyers through the house you find yourself doing a lot of talking and explaining as you describe what they could do with what the house and what it has to offer. You're working really hard to get them to want to buy ... right now!

This time imagine having the house staged to look like an Ethan Allen showroom. The rooms are beautifully furnished and designed, music is playing in the background, and you have chocolate chip cookies baking in the oven. The house "feels" like a home for whomever walks in the door. You don't need to say a word as people walk through the house with smiles on their faces. They see themselves building a life within those four walls. They are already sold.

Although the second scenario requires the investment of time and money to prepare, selling is much easier and ultimately more effective.

Wouldn't it be easier if your potential clients were already "warmed up" and more willing to consider buying personal training services? A qualified customer that is ready to buy is a much easier sale than convincing someone to buy something they don't realize they need.

That's exactly what marketing is designed to do!

Marketing sets the groundwork for all of your sales by preparing your customers to buy. As a result, you spend less time selling and you convert more potential customers to actual clients!

Unfortunately, marketing companies and consultants can be a significant investment for any business (large or small). In an effort to establish themselves in the market, small businesses need marketing assistance the most (to compete against larger, more established fitness businesses) but don't typically have the capital to afford it.

This book (the second book in the "Business of Personal Training" series) is written specifically for fitness entrepreneurs to provide basic marketing knowledge and helpful tools to effectively build their business.

In this book, Part One goes over marketing basics, terminology, and exercises to help businesses establish their brand identity and marketing message. It simplifies marketing concepts and helps fitness business owners identify their unique value to potential customers and shows them how to communicate this message to engage their target audience effectively.

Part Two then goes on to outline sales and marketing strategies and tactics that respect the smaller budgets most personal trainers may have when starting (or growing) their business.

Part Three dives deeper into the power of digital media and the Internet, two areas that are often times misunderstood and underutilized. This section goes over building an effective website and how to leverage the power of social media.

Finally, Part Four outlines sample marketing campaigns specifically developed for the fitness market. These campaigns include grassroots marketing strategies, traditional print marketing and communication tactics through digital and social media.

THE BUSINESS OF PERSONAL TRAINING

Marketing Strategies for the Profitable Personal Trainer

PART ONE:
"MARKETING 101" FOR PERSONAL TRAINERS

Personal trainers have (without a doubt) the best "feel good" job in the world, helping people feel better about themselves and empowering them every day. Unfortunately, the majority of personal trainers also struggle when it comes to making their business financially successful. Very few personal trainers (i.e., Bob Harper, Jillian Michaels, Chris Powell, Harley Pasternak) get the recognition they deserve and make whopping six-figure salaries. Most get into the business for reasons other than fame and fortune, although having a profitable and secure business is a definite bonus!

The majority of personal trainers spend their days, from early morning to late at night, facilitating training sessions and teaching classes for money. A successful, and profitable personal trainer, will schedule an average of six clients/classes per day. A typical day might look like this:

6:00 - 7:00 am	Personal training session
7:00 - 8:00 am	Personal training session
8:00 - 8:30 am	Commute to a different gym location
9:00 - 10:00 am	Teaching a small group training class
10:00 - 10:30 am	Commute to a different gym location
11:00 - 12:00 pm	Phone calls, emails, and food
12:00 - 1:00 pm	Teaching a small group training class
1:00 - 2:00 pm	Free consultation with a new client

2:00 - 4:00 pm	Errands (i.e., picking up the kids)
4:00 - 5:00 pm	Phone calls, emails, and food
5:00 - 6:00 pm	Personal training session
6:00 - 7:00 pm	Personal training session
7:00 - 8:00 pm	Administration (i.e., paperwork, bills, etc.)
8:00 - 10:00 pm	Dinner and free time

With such a busy schedule facilitating sessions, personal trainers spend all of their time "in the business" instead of working "on the business". They feel pressured to train as many clients as they can to earn revenue and fail to spend the time needed to build, grow, and plan for their business's future.

Personal Trainers "Try" to Market Themselves
Whether they've had formal marketing training or not, personal trainers are constantly marketing. Marketing consists of everything you do in order to attract clients to the business. So ... every time they walk out their front door they are marketing themselves to potential clients. This includes:
- Their appearance (i.e., how "fit" they look, the clothes they are wearing)
- How they act
- What they say

Unfortunately, this kind of marketing is limited to the people who might actually be paying attention to you when you are physically in the room (which might only be the one person he/she is training at the time). That marketing strategy is extremely limiting and does not guarantee effective growth or sustainability of the business. Similar to starting a weight training program without a goal, set timeline, or an effective program, getting results is highly unlikely.

Successful personal trainers, on the other hand, take the time to develop a marketing strategy in an effort to:
- Differentiate themselves from the competition
- Generate more revenue (effective marketing campaigns generate more sales)
- Manage their busy schedule effectively

- Develop a more secure and stable business (i.e., consistent client load)

Although this sounds like a tall order, an effective strategy and plan can accomplish all of these things (and more). Financially successful personal trainers don't need extra staff or a marketing company to help them out. They just know how to maximize their time and money to:

"Get the right message to the right audience, at the right time, using the right medium".

By setting aside as little as one hour per day, a personal trainer can build their business and market themselves 24 hours a day, 7 days a week, 365 days a year.

To get you started, the first section of the book is focused on providing information on:
- Marketing (and what it is)
- The different types of marketing media
- The benefits of an effective marketing strategy
- The steps to follow when developing a marketing strategy
- The importance of evaluating your strategy for ongoing growth and success

Are you ready to take your first step into the mystical world of marketing? If so, business will NEVER be the same again!

HERE WE GO!

Chapter 1:
What is Marketing?

Marketing, especially for someone who is passionate about fitness, biomechanics, and anatomy, is a foreign subject that can be really scary and intimidating. To keep it simple, marketing is everything you do to position your fitness (and nutrition) products and personal training services in front of potential clients.

It's an activity, involving a wide variety of actions and strategies that result in making products and services available that satisfy the needs and expectations of customers. The goal is to generate profits for the business. Marketing activities include sales, advertising, public relations, pricing, and packaging. One simple way to explain the differences between each aspect, is with the following anecdote:

> "If a man tells a date she's intelligent, is a great conversationalist, and looks beautiful, he is saying the right things to the right person at the right time, and that is an example of marketing. If the same man tells his date how handsome, smart, and successful he is in business, that's advertising. If someone else tells the young woman (his date) how handsome, smart, and successful her date is, that's an example of public relations."

In any business, whether it be personal training or selling hammers, the goal is to persuade someone to part with their hard earned money. Marketing is all about finding the right people to persuade, by using the right message, at the right time. Therefore, as a business owner, and effective marketing strategy helps you to allocate your valuable time and money to accomplish the following:

1. Generate revenue by selling products and/or services to newly acquired clients
2. Generate revenue by selling products and/or services to existing clients
3. Build client loyalty and repeat business
4. Build client loyalty and referral business
5. Increase the dollar value of each individual sale

Customers Are the Key to Marketing

As simple and calculated as marketing may seem, it really isn't that "cut and dry". Although one would think that marketing begins with a great idea or unique service to sell, it actually starts with customers (the people who will buy what you have to sell). Regardless of how amazing your products or services may be, you need to have an audience of people who want (or need) what you have to sell for your business to succeed.

Most fitness entrepreneurs truly love what they do. Helping people make positive improvements in their lives and getting them to feel better about themselves through fitness and exercise can be "intoxicating". Fitness entrepreneurs also innocently assume everyone else feels the same way about fitness. In reality, the majority of people don't like exercise and are not necessarily looking for what personal trainers have to sell.

People have their own unique perceptions of the world based on their own belief system. For example, if someone is looking to lose weight, but had negative experiences with exercise or sports in school (i.e., embarrassed in gym class, being the last one picked in team sports), they will most likely hesitate when it comes to starting an exercise program at their local gym. Although the program may be proven to work, it will be hard to "sell" this person on the proven weight loss program. In the end, great ideas will only succeed when you market within the context of the perceptions of the people you target.

As a business, you need to market to your customers by fulfilling their wants, providing for their needs, solving their problems, or improving their situation. People don't just "buy" a product or service. They "buy" the concept of what that product or service will do for them, or help them do something for themselves. People who are overweight don't buy a fitness club membership to exercise and get sweaty. They "buy" into the concept of a new, thin, happy, and successful life.

Marketing vs. Selling
Before we continue, let's take a step back and outline the differences between marketing and selling. There is often confusion between the two terms, even though they are very different in their function. Marketing is constantly evolving and changing to meet the needs of various markets. Sales, on the other hand, always stays the same.

Selling consists of the real time conversations between two (or more) people. It happens in the moment and is a short term activity. When it comes to sales, the fundamental motivations for someone to buy, and the skills a salesperson needs to obtain commitments to purchase, will always remain the same. Regardless of what a person purchases, and the various steps they take to buy something, they buy emotionally and justify their decisions intellectually.

Marketing does not involve one-on-one conversations and is a vehicle to broadcast messages to many people at one time (i.e., radio, television, print media, social media, etc.). Unlike a sales transaction, it involves a long term activity designed to deliver a message promising to fulfill a customer's wants and needs through the products and/or services a business has to offer.

Effective marketing strategies, at their core, exploit human psychology. Marketing campaigns target their message to drive consumers to want and/or need a product, by manipulating the thoughts and emotions of the intended audience. These strategies differ based on which medium is used (i.e., television, radio, print media, social media, etc.) and the context of the message. In the end, marketing, when done right, can effectively manipulate a target audience to feel good about purchasing a specific product or service, whether they need it or not.

Marketing Made Simple
There is a common misconception that marketing is for established businesses that have big budgets and a dedicated marketing department. That's why most fitness entrepreneurs (the ones with a passion for fitness and a limited bank account) believe marketing is optional, and something to add to the business when it has the extra money to spend. Being that most fitness entrepreneurs are a "team of one", these business owners are too afraid to tackle marketing on their own and have come to believe they need to hire an expert for marketing to actually work.

Although it is multifaceted, marketing is not a unicorn or mythical creature that is only seen and understood by marketing specialists. Marketing can be broken down into a few basic ingredients, like a successful business "recipe". To keep it simple, marketing consists of the following components:
1. Understanding the "real" demand for a specific product or service
2. Exploring and identifying what motivates clients to buy this product or service
3. Developing a message that makes the purchase more appealing
4. Identifying the ultimate "sweet spot" (where the message, audience, and timing are in perfect harmony)

Understanding the Demand
When it comes to successfully selling personal training or fitness-based services, there needs to be a physical, mental, or emotional desire for what is being sold (i.e., positive health benefits, weight loss, strength gain, improved athletic performance, etc.). Considering more than 69 percent of adults (over the age of 20) are overweight and obese in the United States, the market is definitely in need of what personal trainers have to sell, although this group of people may not realize it. The challenge is developing a compelling message that gets the market to recognize the immediate need, internalize it, and then seek out a solution.

Exploring the Motivations of Personal Training Clients

Motivation, the psychological incentive or reason for doing something, is a key factor that determines why people buy something (i.e., food, clothing, products, services). Motivation can originate from within oneself (intrinsic or internal factors) or from other people or tangible things (extrinsic or external factors).

Internal, or intrinsic, motivation is driven by an interest or enjoyment in the task itself, without the need for any physical reward or recognition. It exists within the individual and is based on taking pleasure in an activity rather than working towards getting "something" for doing it.

Examples of intrinsic motivation, as it relates to exercise and physical activity, includes positive feelings that come from:
- Completing a hard workout
- Reaching a new fitness goal
- The "adrenalin rush" after a long run
- Achieving a new "personal best" time or weight
- Knowing you gave everything you had in your workout (with no regrets)

External, or extrinsic, motivation comes from outside of the individual and is not under their control. In this scenario, people are motivated to take action in an effort to earn a reward (i.e., money, prizes, material things), gain recognition or to avoid punishment.

Examples of extrinsic motivation, as it relates to exercise and physical activity, includes:
- Rewarding yourself with a shopping spree when you lose ten pounds
- Showing up at the gym every day to impress someone you're attracted to (who is also there at the same time)
- Joining the company running team to fit in with your colleagues
- Starting an exercise program because your doctor said you are at high risk of type 2 diabetes and coronary heart disease

Regardless of whether a personal training client is intrinsically or extrinsically motivated, the way you communicate the value of your services to each will be different. For example, a woman signed up for a bridal bootcamp class may be motivated by the idea of feeling "beautiful" and "confident" on her wedding day, while another woman may want to avoid the embarrassment of being too big to fit into her wedding gown.

In the end, it's important to develop marketing strategies that speak to different personality types and the "hot buttons" that get each of them to purchase your services.

Developing the Right Message

The goal of every marketing message is to effectively connect your products and services to something that your target audience genuinely cares about. People don't care about your or your business. They care about the benefits they get when they purchase from you. To successfully deliver a strong marketing message, you need to ask yourself the following questions:

1. Who is my target market?
2. What are the "pain" points, issues, needs, and wants of my potential clients? How will my personal training business addresses them?
3. How do I briefly describe the products and/or services I offer?
4. What are my "proof" points (that prove my business can overcome these needs)?
5. What makes me different from my competitors?
6. What messaging platform(s) will be the most effective?

To move your potential clients into action you need to take a step back, identify their problems, issues, needs, and wants, and define how your business (without question) addresses each one of these concerns. In the next chapter, you will learn more about marketing messages and applying them to your marketing strategies.

Identifying the "Sweet Spot"

According to the Harvard Business Review, the strategic sweet spot of a company is "where it meets a customer's needs in a way that competitors can't, given the context in which it competes". In other words, the sweet spot is delivering the right message to the right audience at the right time (when the competition doesn't interfere).

Because the fitness industry is predictable, planning effective marketing campaigns is easier than for other industries that are continually in a state of flux (i.e., stock market and investments, oil and gas, real estate). The summer months typically represent the slowest time of year for fitness sales. People would much rather spend their time soaking up the sun, taking summer vacations, and participating in outdoor activities. On the other hand, the colder months (starting in September, peaking in January, and ending in April) are where people are focused on staying out of the cold, avoiding the "holiday bulge", and getting their bodies ready for a summer time reveal.

Speaking in general terms, the target market for personal trainers are individuals who need help improving various aspects of their fitness and health and (at some point) are ready to make a change. These individuals are looking to learn new skills in order to improve their overall health and longevity, and fall into one of the following categories:

1. Their health is compromised and they are unaware of the problem (i.e., unconscious incompetence).
2. Their health is compromised (or they have a specific health and/ or fitness goal), they know they have a problem and need help to make a change (i.e., conscious incompetence).
3. Their health is compromised (or they have a specific health and/ or fitness goal), they know they have a problem and need help to make a change, and are actively learning skills to improve their situation (i.e., conscious incompetence).
4. Their health was compromised (or they had a specific health and/or fitness goal) and they have learned the skills necessary to change their situation that are now "second nature" (i.e., conscious competence).

As a fitness entrepreneur, your mission (should you choose to accept it) is to develop targeted messages for each of the above "potential" clients in an effort to move each one closer to becoming a client of your services.

Are you **READY** for the challenge?

Chapter 2:
Developing the "Right" Marketing Message

Now that you have a better understanding of what marketing is, and its importance for your growing personal training business, let's start with one of the most important first steps ... your marketing message.

The primary marketing message for your business essentially describes your business to the world. It's meant to communicate the story behind your brand identity (i.e., the visible elements of a brand, such as colors, design, logotype and/or symbol), what you offer as a service provider and your overall business value to the customer.

Because it takes a little bit of time and thought to get your primary marketing message right, many business owners fall back on the "About Us" page on their website or product descriptions to explain what they do and for whom. The problem with this approach is that the information is focused on the business and not about the people you are trying to attract ... your customers.

Just like a stable house needs a good foundation to build upon, so does your marketing. A strong marketing platform (which includes your marketing, positioning and brand statements) is essential for any business, to ensure your brand "story" is communicated consistently and confidently to your customers.

The following steps will help you carefully think about your business, gather the information needed, and construct effective marketing, positioning and brand statements for your business.

1. Understand Your Target Market

The ultimate goal of marketing is to effectively "connect" with your target market. The words you choose in your marketing message must resonate with the specific demographic of people who are best suited for the products and services you offer (i.e., supervised fitness and exercise instruction). Ask yourself:

- What am I selling and to whom?
- Am I clearly communicating the benefits of doing business with me?
- Are these benefits important to the target market?

If the benefits you've outlined do not match the needs of the target market, you may need to re-evaluate the target market to determine the fit for your business.

For example, if you're a competitive triathlete, who is known for your rigorous training regime and winning track record, going after the first time fitness participant or medically supervised weight loss market might not be a good fit. These clients may feel intimidated and reluctant to train with someone who is known for extreme workouts and pushing themselves to the limit.

In this situation, a demographic that matches the passions and training style of this personal trainer may be proactive, goal-oriented individuals looking to achieve aggressive weight loss goals or aspiring triathletes looking for a good role model to work with.

2. Know Your Customer's "Pain Points"

The goal of any business is to provide a solution to a problem. These are the "pain points" you need to identify to ensure you communicate the innate value of your business as a provider of solutions to these problems. Examples of pain points include:

- A challenge that is not easily overcome (i.e., getting lost and safely arriving at your destination)

- A need that requires fulfilment (i.e., something that is needed for survival - food, water, shelter or companionship)
- A desire that needs satisfying (i.e., something that is not necessary for survival - chocolate, a new pair of shoes or outfit).

For some businesses, like an auto repair shop, the pain points are obvious. When it comes to a fitness business the pain points are a bit harder to define. For example, a fitness business is rarely considered a "superhero or life saver". An amazing exercise program won't stop an open wound or solve any life threatening problems needing immediate attention. But you can certainly develop a benefit statement out of the fact that, with the help of a knowledgeable personal trainer, you can achieve your weight loss goals faster and with better results. Working with a personal trainer provides you with the tools that help to you be successful, including:
- Motivation
- Accountability
- Knowledge and experience
- Exercise programs that work
- Nutrition programs that work
- Guidance for lifelong weight management

If you can effectively highlight someone's pain points (i.e., that they have a health and fitness goal they want to achieve, but can't do it on their own) it is easy to drive the need and desire to acquire what you have to offer.

3. Explain Your Product - Be Clear and Brief
Products (and services) are a key part of what you do as a personal trainer, but they don't represent everything. The actual product or service that you bring to your target audience should only represent a small part of the overall experience of a client working with you. For example, as a personal trainer, aside from providing personal training services, you also offer knowledge and experience, reliability, exceptional customer service and genuine care. Consider all of these added values and what they might mean to your customer. Why would any of these matter to a client and what benefit does it bring to them?

4. Add Proof Points

A "proof point" backs up any statement you make about your personal training business from an outside source. They include client testimonials, before and after photos showing physical results, articles written about your business by the media, and references. These "proof points" are important because they show how your business has solved the problems of others and have earned the respect of their peers. In just a few words, or paragraphs, a potential client can relate to a customer's challenge, how you provided a solution, and the results they achieved with your help.

5. Determine How You are Different

Any good business idea is going to have competition. The more competition you come across simply validates you are in a business that is bound to make money! Unfortunately, that also means you have to work harder to get noticed amongst the crowd of personal trainers going after the same target market!

In order to differentiate yourself from the competition, think about what makes you unique as a personal trainer and as a business operator. Try to tie these differences to a perceived value. For example, if you were a former competitive athlete who suffered a career ending injury a client wanting help rehabilitating post-surgery may want to work with someone who can relate to their pain and frustration with the rehabilitation process.

Identify the reasons "why" a potential client would care about what you do versus your competitor?

6. Developing Your Messaging Platform

Now that you've taken the time to think about, and gathered information on, your business it's time to develop the various components of your messaging platform:
- Vision statement
- Mission statement
- Positioning statement
- Elevator statement
- Key messages

16

Vision Statement

A Vision Statement exists to inform other people involved with your business (i.e., partners, investors or staff) the future vision for the personal training business. It's a statement that speaks to the future, typically 3 to five years, the clearly outlines where you want to go with the business. Using ACTIV Personal Training, a sport-specific training and conditioning provider, an example of a Vision Statement could be:

To be the most sought after sport-specific training and conditioning provider in Denver, CO.

Mission Statement

While your Vision Statement guides where you want your business to be in 3 to 5 years, your Mission Statement clarifies your reason for existing and helps to focus the actions involved in running your business. Your mission is the reason "why" you go to work everyday as a personal trainer. Your Mission Statement should establish "how you accomplish your mission" as a personal training business.

For example, if you want to become the most sought after sport-specific training and conditioning provider in Denver, CO your mission could be to help aspiring athletes achieve the highest level in their sport. An example of a Mission Statement, that supports fulfilling the mission each and every day, could be:

To provide the highest quality sport-specific programs, using scientifically proven and rigorously tested techniques and protocols, designed to achieve measurable results.

Positioning Statement

The positioning statement is essentially your marketing statement. It outlines, very clearly and succinctly, what you do better than anyone else as a personal training business. This statement should answer the following questions:

- What do you do?
- Who do you do it for?
- Why is your approach different from the competition?
- What will they get out of it?

This is not necessarily an easy task. Use the following business template: *[YOUR COMPANY]* provides *[PRIMARY PRODUCT/SERVICE]* for *[PRIMARY AUDIENCE]*. Unlike *[YOUR COMPETITOR]*, *[YOUR COMPANY]* makes the world a better place by *[YOUR PRIMARY POINT OF DIFFERENCE]*.

For the Positioning Statement, the point is not to state why you are better, it is to clearly communicate why you are different or special. An example of a Mission Statement could be:

ACTIV Personal Training provides sport-specific training and conditioning services for elite athletes and individuals proactively looking to perform at their very best. Unlike traditional fitness clubs or studios, ACTIV Personal Training is actively involved in their community by coordinating fund raisers in support of local amateur sport organizations and providing training camps for underprivileged youth in Denver, CO.

Elevator Statement

Unlike the Positioning Statement, which is another internal statement used for you (and the people involved in your business), the Elevator Statement is an external statement that communicates to potential clients exactly "what your personal training business does". The Elevator Statement is a quick statement that can be SPOKEN between the floors of an elevator ride. Because it is a spoken statement, it needs to use conversational language that doesn't sound like "marketing language". Anyone who represents your business should be able to deliver it comfortably in a natural conversation (i.e., your partners, other trainers, your family, existing clients, etc.). Imagine describing your personal training business to your parents and the language you would use to explain to them what your business does. An example of an Elevator Statement could be:

We train athletes who are serious about performance. Regardless of the sport we develop programs for individuals and teams using the coolest technologies and gadgets to measure performance and results. Are you familiar with the NFL combine? The stuff you see them do at those events are along the lines of the type of training we

include in our sport-specific programs ... but with a technology twist!

Key Messages (or Talking Points)

Beyond the Elevator Statement, if someone gives you more time to explain what you do, what are the 3 to 5 messages you want everyone to know about your personal training business? These are your Key Messages, and most important facts, you need to communicate about your business to the world. They should be documented and referenced in all of your communications and advertising platforms (i.e., print, websites, articles, social media, etc.). An example of Key Messages could be:

- *ACTIV Personal Training offers state-of-the-art technologies and protocols used by the professional athletes and amateur athletes at the highest level of their sport.*
- *ACTIV Personal Training develops sport-specific training programs that are focused on both improved performance and injury prevention.*
- *ACTIV Personal Training is a proud sponsor of local amateur sport organizations, coordinates fund raisers and offers training camps for underprivileged youth in Denver, CO.*
- *ACTIV Personal Training sponsors a scholarship that assists one student per year enrolled in the Kinesiology program at University of Colorado.*

As a whole, your messaging platform needs to allow for flexibility, without sacrificing the impact of a consistent message. You should be able to change the messaging to suit your audience, your collateral (i.e., brochure, website, proposal, social media, etc.), a promotion or sales pitch.

A common practice is to create 25, 50 and 100 word versions of your message. Shorter versions can be used for advertising, sound bites or elevator pitches, while longer versions give you more flexibility to add specific services, benefits and situation-specific examples of why potential clients should train with your company.

7. Use Your Messaging Consistently

Once you have your business messaging developed, make sure

everyone involved in the operation of your personal training business is well versed and communicating the same message. The more your clients (and potential clients) hear the same message the more likely it will resonate with them, in addition to consolidating your personal training brand in the marketplace.

The development of your marketing platform is a process that you should dedicate time to and involve the people who play a significant role in your business. You DO NOT want to do this exercise alone, nor do you want to cut corners. This task sets the foundation for the success of your business and alleviates any potential uncertainty as your business grows, expands and evolves over time.

ACTIV PERSONAL TRAINING
- DEVELOPING THE RIGHT MESSAGE -

My Target Market:
1. Athletes (all abilities) looking to improve their performance
2. Individuals who have just undergone surgery (orthopedic) and are looking to get back into shape

My Products & Services:
- Sport-specific training and conditioning (one-on-one, small group and team training)
- TRX Suspension Training and TRX RIP Training
- FitLight Trainer
- Assessments and Testing

"Pain" Points of the Client:
- Exercise isn't fun
- Starting an exercise program doesn't always guarantee success

"Proof" Points of the Business:
- Testimonials of past and current clients
- Endorsements from high profile athletes and coaches

Business Differentiators:
- Focus on sports performance and athlete development
- Highly specialized personal trainers, strength and conditioning coaches, athletic trainers and sports performance specialists
- Use of innovative technologies for measurable results
- Focus on science-based solutions and producing results

How the Message is Delivered
- One-on-one
- Print media (brochures, flyers, signage, etc.)
- Website
- Social media

Figure 2-1: Developing the Right Message (Sample for ACTIV Personal Training)

Chapter 3:
Types of Marketing

In order for your personal training business to stay "top of mind" in a very competitive industry, you need to consider many types of marketing strategies to get the best results.

A good marketing strategy effectively communicates, to a target market, the benefits and features of your products and services. Although you have a very specific target market as your focus, you need to accept the fact that there you need to accommodate varying communication styles and that it is highly unlikely you will attract everyone's attention with a single marketing campaign.

Marketing strategies can also communicate an overall value to your potential clients. In many cases, this is the core of building good equity or good will in your target markets. For example, Samsung has invested in creating commercials for television, billboards and magazines that showcased their products in such a way that their customers feel a connection towards Samsung products.

Below are examples of various types of marketing that can be used to help grow and increase product and service sales for your personal training business.

1. Cause Marketing

Finding a cause both you and your customers care about can create a magnetic connection for your business. This requires a good understanding of what you personally (as the owner of the business) care about and how you want to help the community, nation or world. For example, the Susan G. Komen Race for the Cure® is an event that connects people whose lives have been affected by breast cancer. As a personal trainer, you could work with the organizers of a local 5K event by offering to donate your time, guiding the runners through a warm up at the start of the race and a cool down after the race. This will expose you and your personal training brand to like-minded people who may also be looking for your services.

2. Content Marketing

Very few people will purchase personal training without doing a little bit of research on it first. Content marketing involves the writing and publishing of content on your website (or other credible websites) to educate potential customers about your products and services. For personal trainers this is an extremely effective way to influence potential customers without having to use direct selling methods.

3. Direct Mail Marketing

This is essentially marketing that speaks directly to the customer and covers a wide range of strategies. Typically a marketing message is directed to a potential customer to create an action response (i.e., call now, buy now, visit our website) using email, text messaging, consumer websites, online display ads, printed fliers, promotional letters and outdoor advertising.

4. Email Marketing

Email has made it much faster, easier and cost effective to connect with qualified buyers looking for your services. Assuming that you have a database of names and email addresses of people who have given you permission to communicate with them (i.e., your past or current clients, opt-in list from your website, etc.) you can easily broadcast to thousands of emails at a time using online tools like Constant Contact, MailChimp or iContact. Examples of broadcast emails to your database include: monthly newsletter, current promotions, or holidays greetings.

5. Event Marketing

Creating events (or a promotion that is tied to calendar holiday) is a great way to drive sales. For example, offering a "Thanksgiving Pre-Dinner Bootcamp" is a perfect way to provide a guilt-free solution on a day where most people consume excess calories and (often times) feel guilty afterwards.

6. Freebie Marketing

Let's face it. Everybody likes FREE stuff! One way to gain new clients is by giving away a complimentary service (i.e., fitness assessment, customized program, copy of your published book, etc.) with the purchase of a higher ticket item (i.e., 10 or 20 personal training sessions).

7. Guerrilla (or Grassroots) Marketing

Guerrilla marketing, also known as "grassroots marketing", is an advertising strategy that focuses on low-cost, unconventional marketing tactics that yield maximum results. This type of marketing is about taking the consumer by surprise, making a lasting impact, and creating a lot of social buzz about your business. For example, staging a push up contest in the parking lot of a local shopping center to win three personal training sessions for a friend or family member.

8. Online Marketing

The Internet has become a powerful medium to educate people about your business, promote your brand, and entice online shoppers to buy (if you sell personal training services and/or programs on your website). Most online strategic marketing efforts include paid advertising (i.e., Google Ads, social media ads, etc.) and awareness tactics that drive attention to your website.

9. Promotional Marketing

Promotional marketing is a business marketing strategy designed to motivate a customer to take action towards a buying decision. This type of marketing includes various incentives to buy. Examples include contests (buy and enter to win the grand prize), coupons (percentage discount on all purchases within a specific timeline), and sampling (free group fitness class to showcase the exercise experience before they buy).

10. Relationship Marketing

In a service-based industry, like personal training, relationship marketing is essential to building and developing your personal training brand. Unlike a business that sells products in a retail environment, personal training businesses are built on relationships that involve respect and trust. Relationship marketing would include activities that foster long-term relationships, brand loyalty and customer retention. This involves knowing a clients likes/dislikes, tailoring an experience to their needs, and customizing their offering to make their interactions unique and unforgettable.

11. Social Media Marketing

Social media marketing programs focus on creating content that attracts attention and encourages readers to share this information across their social networks. This is an example of "electronic word-of-mouth" that spreads a message about your business in a positive way that can help it grow. For example, posting a "before and after" picture of a client (with their consent) who lost 50 pounds working with you may motivate others to find you to help them achieve the same results.

12. Word-of-Mouth Marketing

People who are impressed by a product or service are excited to tell others about their experiences. The sharing of information from one person to another is "word-of-mouth marketing". People find meaning in sharing stories of their favorite products and services. Because people tend to buy from businesses they trust, the endorsement of others is a motivating force.

Final Thoughts

Regardless of the types of marketing you choose for your business, be sure to include a wide variety of strategies and tactics to get the best response for your efforts. It will take time to test out different strategies to determine which ones are right for you. Also, be sure to evaluate each strategy to determine which ones are the most effective so they can be used time and time again!

Chapter 4:
Marketing Doesn't Exist Without Media

Now that you have a basic understanding of how marketing works, the next step is to choose the right medium (or vehicle) for your marketing message. There are hundreds of ways to market (or advertise) but only a few will be suitable for personal trainers.

In general, there are four types of marketing media:
1. Broadcast
2. Print
3. Digital and interactive
4. Social media

Broadcast
Broadcast media includes television and radio. Of the two, radio is generally the more affordable option for a small business, as you can often get a few hundred ads for as little as $1,000. Television offers more impact for the target audience, but it can cost as much as $10,000 to $25,000 for a small-market commercial.

Print
Print media refers to anything printed on paper and physically handed out. Newspapers and magazines are the most recognized forms of traditional print media, but it also includes catalogs, brochures, handouts,

and flyers. Newspapers are very affordable for small businesses and are useful in a local market. Unfortunately, newspaper circulation is not as popular in recent years with the availability of the Internet and digital media. Magazines offer high selectivity and audience interest because of their niche topics, though costs are usually higher than newspapers, even in local markets.

Examples of print media include:
- Newspapers
- Magazines
- Newsletters
- Banners and posters
- Billboards
- Direct mail
- Brochures
- Flyers

Although the cost of a radio spot, television commercial, or print advertisement may be unrealistic with a limited budget, you can still leverage the power of broadcast and print marketing. Local television, radio stations, and newspapers love to highlight "human interest" stories. As you build your network, and circle of influence, look for opportunities to highlight what you do for your community and clients as a guest speaker for local shows or for interviews in a printed article. You can get the exposure of an expensive commercial without the cost, if you provide value to the these news providers.

Digital and Interactive

The newest marketing medium, digital and interactive, use computer-based systems to present content (i.e., text, graphics, animation, video, audio, games, etc.). It utilizes the Internet, email, and mobile devices (i.e., smartphones and tablets). With the emergence of the Internet in the 1990s (and our growing reliance on getting information ... FAST), businesses are leveraging the marketing power of the world wide web. The Internet provides a platform to share information all day, all night, and all year long. Banner ads, streaming audio and video, and web-based media messages have become common practices for small businesses looking to leverage a small budget, yet reach a high volume of people. Email serves as a way to directly market compelling images and messages to existing customers (including newsletters and targeted promotions) and mobile devices have expanded the opportunities for targeted marketing to large groups of people at a moment's notice.

Social Media

Social media, which has been evolving since the early 21st century, offers a low-cost way for personal trainers to engage their clients in a more personal and targeted way. Social media sites (i.e., Facebook, Twitter, Google+, Instagram, YouTube and Pinterest) offer free accounts that let users create, share, and exchange information online. In today's fast-paced, technology-driven marketplace, social media is essential for personal trainers looking to grow their business. You can send out messages to all followers via Twitter, but also respond directly to individual comments and discussions. Facebook allows for event pages, announcements, question-and-answer posts, and other ongoing interactions with clients. As technology improves in the years to come, this medium may make others obsolete.

Examples of social media platforms include:
- Facebook (www.facebook.com)
- Flickr (www.flickr.com)
- Google+ (www.plus.google.com)
- Instagram (www.instagram.com)
- LinkedIn (www.linkedin.com)
- MeetUp (www.meetup.com)
- Pinterest (www.pinterest.com)
- Tumblr (www.tumblr.com)
- Twitter (www.twitter.com)
- YouTube (www.youtube.com)

Choosing the Right Media

Choosing the which media to use for your advertising campaigns depends on four factors:
1. Your objective
2. Your target audience

3. Your message (and frequency)
4. Your budget

Marketing Objective

The marketing objective is "what you want to accomplish and by when". Knowing what you want to accomplish is critical for the success of your marketing efforts. Examples of marketing objectives include:

- Increasing sales
- Improving awareness of your products and services
- Establishing credibility (i.e., your community, the fitness industry)
- Increasing awareness of your personal and/or business brand

Target Audience

In order to identify your target audience you need to know "who" they are and "where" to reach them. Certain media will have stronger appeal to some groups than others. Narrowing down your audience will help you make wise and cost-efficient media choices. For example, if you were promoting a Bridal Bootcamp program, targeting women between the ages of 25 and 40 years, media that could get good exposure include:

- Print advertisements in a local bridal magazine
- Flyers at the local specialty bake shop
- Brochures provided to a local wedding planner
- A blog post promoting the program on your website
- A "Bridal Bootcamp" board on Pinterest
- A "Bridal Bootcamp" Facebook page

By understanding the needs and habits of your target audience, you can focus the message to get a better overall response.

Message Content and Frequency

Choosing the most effective medium depends on the type of information you need to share, how much content the audience needs to absorb, and how often you need to broadcast it. For example, if you have a lot of information to broadcast, a 30 second radio spot wouldn't be a good idea. A flyer or brochure may be more suitable. In another example, a printed flyer of a written testimonial isn't nearly as powerful as a YouTube video showing the before and after images of your client, including a voice recording of their testimonial. This could be a powerful tool to generate a response when people visit your website.

When it comes to frequency, choose a medium that meets the timeline of the message. For example, if a personal training package promotion is ending in two days, using print media will take too long to produce and won't be distributed in time. A broadcast email and posts on Facebook and Twitter would be more appropriate. Keep in mind, social media platforms inherently involve a lot of "noise" (your message is up against hundreds of others at any given time). Your post needs to catch their attention and should be posted multiple times to get the best response.

Marketing Budget

Your budget is probably the single most influential factor in planning your marketing and advertising. Marketing media costs can vary depending on which avenue you use. There is an inverse relationship between the cost of the media and the amount of work you are required to do. Typically, the more you pay for the media, the less physical work you need to do. For example, television and radio cost the most, but require very little work by the personal trainer.

The reverse is also true. For example, printed flyers and brochures require a small investment but need to be physically distributed to get into the hands of the target audience. Social media is essentially "free" but you need to be communicating through them on a daily basis to remain relevant, the messages (including images and video) require very strategic thought, and they need to be posted multiple times to get a good response.

When looking at the budget, take into account the cost of both the marketing materials and the additional time it will take to distribute the message.

Final Thoughts

Remember, the marketing medium (whichever one you choose) is the only way to deliver your marketing message. Be sure to choose the medium carefully because the wrong one could end up costing more money than you make in the end.

Chapter 5:
Developing an Effective Marketing Campaign

Just like an effective personal training program, a marketing campaign requires a goal, strategies and tactics, a budget, and a timeline. A well planned marketing campaign can be simplified into five steps:

1. Analyze the situation
2. Target the right audience
3. Define the goal(s) of the campaign
4. Create strategies and tactics
5. Establish a realistic budget

By following each of these steps, you can outline a plan for success that ensures the valuable time, money, and effort you put in results in growing your personal training business.

Analyze the Situation

Before you start any marketing campaign, it's important to evaluate your current situation.

- What are your current products and services?
- What marketing advantages and challenges do you face?
- What threats are posed by your competitors?

By knowing where you are starting from, you can outline strategies that are relevant to your business "today" and you can establish goals that are realistic.

Target the Right Audience

Personal training is something that could be utilized by people of all ages and abilities. There are very few people who can't benefit from the services you offer. Unfortunately, a marketing campaign should target a very specific group of people for the greatest effect (especially if you have a limited budget). First determine whether you want to market to your current clients, new prospects, or both. Regardless, it is important to identify your target audience by outlining demographic data, including:

- Age
- Gender
- Ethnicity
- Languages
- Location

This information is important because it will determine the what content you choose that will best "speak" to the target audience (i.e., words, images, colors) for the greatest overall effect.

Define the Goal(s) of the Campaign

List the goals you wish to accomplish for this particular marketing campaign. To be effective they need to be specific, measurable, attainable, realistic, and time bound (S.M.A.R.T.). Examples of goals include:

- Sell a minimum of ten personal training packages in the next 30 days
- Gain brand recognition in the local community
- Get a minimum of four referrals from current clients
- Establish relationships with at minimum of two corporations interested in onsite personal training services

These are an important part of the evaluation process at the end of a marketing campaign to determine if it was successful and if it can be used again at another time (with guaranteed results).

Create Strategies and Tactics

This section will take up the majority of your time and creative thought. A strategy is the overall plan and tactics are the actions that work towards achieving an outlined goal. Tactics include all the actionable steps you plan to take for advertising, public relations, direct mail, trade shows, and special promotions.

For example, if a goal is to sell five weight loss programs in the month of January, a strategy would be to establish a discounted rate for the program during the month, and tactics could include mailing a one-page promotional piece to all current customers and broadcasting an email to your complete opt-in database list.

Be sure to properly schedule each of the tactics, including the correct sequence of actions (i.e., the website should be updated before sending out a broadcast email that includes a link to the promotional website page).

In the end, strategies and tactics are only as good as your willingness to put the plan into action.

Establish a Realistic Budget

No matter how great a marketing campaign may be on paper, without the funds to make it happen ... it will do nothing to help your business. Most small businesses, including personal trainers, allocate limited funds to marketing. Even though the funds are limited, it doesn't mean that you have to sacrifice tactics that you've included in your plan. What it does mean is that you may not be able to go as big in scale as you had hoped. For example, you may have planned to send a direct mail piece to a target audience within a 10 mile radius. If your budget doesn't allow for this you can decrease the reach to a five mile radius to stay on budget. The tactics are still helpful to your business, you just won't reach as many people.

Evaluating Your Marketing Campaign

Most people don't like getting evaluated, for fear of being judged by others (or ourselves). Regardless, it's an opportunity for a business to learn and grow. You get a chance to determine:

- Your performance in relation to the goal (i.e., hit it, missed it, or

exceeded expectations)
- What you did well
- What you could improve on

If the marketing campaign is successful, you can take information from the evaluation and improve on it for future use. Like they say, "If it ain't broke, don't fix it".

Final Thoughts
Marketing, a necessary part of running a personal training business, is more than just handing out business cards or talking to people about your business. It is a collection of activities that involve creating, communicating, and delivering products and services that your potential clients value. The overall goal is to:

> *"Get the right message to the right audience, at the right time, using the right medium."*

As great as this all sounds, it's likely you are feeling overwhelmed with all of the information you've read so far. That's totally understandable! Luckily, there is a section dedicated to outlining marketing ideas and samples that put all of these concepts and ideas into action!

Chapter 6:
Evaluating the Marketing Campaign

When it comes to any marketing campaign, the most challenging part is taking the time to objectively evaluate whether or not it was successful. Granted, if you were running large company with employees dedicated to marketing ... this would be easy. This select group of people would have the experience and "know how" to let you know what went well, what needs work and let you know when to run the campaign again in the future. Unfortunately, you're business is most likely run as a sole proprietorship (an unincorporated business owned and run by one individual, with distinction between the business and the owner), and you have to do this all by yourself!

It's not that you can't learn the right marketing principles or evaluation techniques ... it's that self-evaluation is just HARD TO DO (in one's personal life and in business).

For any business owner, the business naturally becomes personal and how it performs is often times perceived as a direct reflection of self-worth and confidence. If the business is not doing well, it's hard to feel good about oneself.

Regardless, evaluation and analysis is essential for any business to be successful, grow consistently and stay competitive in the market.

Asking the RIGHT Questions

The definition of "evaluation" is:

"A systematic determination of a subject's merit, worth and significance, using criteria governed by a set of standards. It can assist an organization, program, project or any other intervention or initiative to assess the degree of achievement in regard to the objectives and results of any such action that is completed."

The criteria and set standards are based on the specific goals you set for each marketing campaign you run. To help you make good business decisions, and to avoid costly mistakes, be sure to establish S.M.A.R.T. goals (as referenced in the previous chapter) and ask yourself the following questions in advance:

1. What target audience will the marketing campaign be directed towards?
2. What is a realistic sales goal for my marketing campaign?
3. What is a realistic budget for this marketing campaign?
4. Will this marketing campaign generate sufficient profits to be worth making the investment (of time and money)?
5. What is the projected audience size?
6. In order to accomplish this reach, what types of media will be used?
7. What is my marketing cost per contact?
8. How many new clients are necessary to reach my sales goal?

Once the campaign is completed, it's now time to evaluate the marketing campaign with a different set of questions:

1. Did you reach your sales goal? Why or why not?
2. Did this campaign result in the sales of other products and/or services? Explain.
3. Were you able to stay within budget? Why or why not?
4. Provide a general description of the clients who bought the promoted product or service.
5. Did the marketing tools grab the attention of the target audience? Why or why not?
6. Is this target audience particularly profitable for my business?

Why or why not?

7. How many hours did you personally dedicate to this marketing campaign? Did the marketing campaign consume too much time (keeping you from running your personal training business)?

8. Considering the amount of time you dedicated to running this campaign, would you consider hiring outside assistance (i.e., advertising agency)? Why or why not?

9. Identify three (3) things done well in this campaign. Explain.

10. Identify three (3) things to improve on for future deliveries of this campaign. Explain.

SAMPLE - Lululemon SeaWheeze Half Marathon (August 2016)

ACTIV Personal Training is dedicated to helping our clients achieve measurable results. Our experienced and knowledgeable staff provide the motivation, education, and personal attention needed to help people achieve their goals. Whether you are looking to lose five pounds or win an Olympic medal ... we have the commitment, compassion and care to help you every step of the way!

In preparation for the Lululemon SeaWheeze Half Marathon (August 2016) we are offering our annual "12 Week Half Marathon Training Program" (starting May 1, 2016). This comprehensive program includes the following:

- 12 week running schedule (4-5 days/week)
- Weekly one-on-one training session (60 minutes)
- Weekly group training session and education (60 minutes)
- Comprehensive fitness assessment
- Comprehensive nutrition assessment and 12 week customized healthy eating plan
- Stretching program
- 20% Discount at Running World

The cost of the complete program is $1,250.00 (value of $1,750.00).

PRELIMINARY QUESTIONS:

1. What target audience will the marketing campaign be directed towards?
    - *Individuals who are interested in training for their first half*

marathon and/or participate in the Lululemon SeaWheeze Half Marathon.

2. What is a realistic sales goal for my marketing campaign?
   - *$10,000.00*
3. What is a realistic budget for this marketing campaign?
   - *$1,600.00*
4. Will this marketing campaign generate sufficient profits to be worth making the investment (of time and money)?
   - *Yes. The summer months (May to August) are the slowest months of the year. This campaign will generate $8,600.00 in profit (sold in 30 days) and keep the schedule busy until September.*
5. What is the projected audience size?
   - *Current email database of 2,800+ email addresses, 200+ addresses (all established contacts), and 200 face-to-face contacts (projected)*
6. To accomplish this sales goal, what types of media will be used?
   - *Website, email broadcast, mailed letter, guest speaker at a local health fair, and hosting a free stretching workshop at the YMCA (for runners)*
7. What is my marketing cost per contact?
   - *$0.50 per contact*
8. How many programs are necessary to reach my sales goal?
   - *8 programs (8 x $1,250 = $10,000)*

EVALUATION OF THE CAMPAIGN

Start Date:	**April 1, 2016**
End Date:	**April 30, 2016**
Sales Revenue (actual):	**$ 14,500.00**
Marketing Budget (actual):	**$ 3,100.00**
Profit (actual):	**$ 11,400.00**

1. Did you reach your sales goal? Why or why not?
   - *Yes and no. During the month of April ACTIV Personal Training exceeded the $10,000 sales goal, but ended up with 13 program participants (making the average sale $1,115.39 versus $1,250.00). The rationale for the price decrease was because only 6 programs were sold with 5 days left in the*

month and the program price was dropped to $1,000.00. This resulted in 7 sales in 5 days.

2. Did this campaign result in the sales of other products and/or services? Explain.
    - *Yes. Three of the program clients also purchased the Isagenix® Energy & Performance Pak for the duration of the 12 week program (3 x $1,000.00 = $3,000.00; $1,000 in profit). Two other people signed up for the Lululemon SeaWheeze Half Marathon and each purchased a 5-Pack (2 x $350.00 = $700.00) of sessions instead.*

3. Were you able to stay within budget? Why or why not?
    - *No. Because the price of the program was dropped by $250.00 with 5 days left to go. This increases the marketing budget by $1,500.00.*

4. Provide a general description of the clients who bought the promoted product or service.
    - *Although ACTIV Personal Training's clients are traditionally high performance athletes and "Weekend Warriors", 65 percent of the program participants had never run a distance further than one mile. The majority of the participants were between the ages of 35 and 50 years of age.*

5. Did the marketing tools grab the attention of the target audience? Why or why not?
    - *Yes. The personalized letter generated 3 sales (from 5 inbound calls), the email blast led to 150 clicks to the website (which generated 4 sales online) and the Facebook ad resulted in one program purchase. The remaining 5 programs were as a result of face-to-face interactions that led to a sale.*

6. Is this target audience particularly profitable for my business? Why or why not?
    - *Yes and no. We exceeded our sales goals but had to drop the prices even further to make sales. The typical cost of a single personal training session is $95.00 (for 60 minutes). This demographic is less likely to pay full price for the elite level personal training services and (most likely) will not purchase beyond this value-added program.*

7. How many hours did you personally dedicate to this marketing campaign? Did the marketing campaign consume too much time

(keeping you from running your personal training business)?

- *During the preparation of the campaign (prior to April 1st) more than 40 of my personal hours were dedicated to the creation of marketing pieces, strategy development and implementation. Any business or administrative task that takes 10+ hours is not an effective use of my time or ability to generate revenue.*

8. Considering the amount of time you dedicated to running this campaign, would you consider hiring outside assistance (i.e., advertising agency)? Why or why not?

- *Yes. A marketing expert could have completed the work in one quarter of the time and at a much higher standard.*

9. Identify three (3) things done well in this campaign. Explain.

- *Crafted the right message to the "non-athletic" person (ages 35 to 50 years) wanting to run their first half marathon.*
- *Adjusted the pricing to adapt the service offering and value for the interested demographic.*
- *Provided a good "pitch" during grassroots events in the community (creating a high close ratio).*

10. Identify three (3) things to improve on for future deliveries of this campaign. Explain.

- *Adjust the messaging to target an older demographic that is willing to pay suggested retail price (and not having to discount).*
- *Start the campaign sooner (March 15th; adding two more weeks).*
- *Include one more grassroots marketing event for one-on-one interaction and sales opportunities (highest close ratio).*

Final Thoughts

Regardless of the outcome of any marketing campaign (no matter how successful it may "seem") you have an opportunity to learn from your actions and correct your mistakes. The choice is yours.

ACTIV PERSONAL TRAINING
- SMART GOALS & EVALUATING THE CAMPAIGN -

Planning the Campaign
1. What target audience will the marketing campaign be directed towards?
2. What is a realistic sales goal for my marketing campaign?
3. What is a realistic budget for this marketing campaign?
4. Will this marketing campaign generate sufficient profits to be worth making the investment (of time and money)?
5. What is the projected audience size?
6. In order to accomplish this reach, what types of media will be used?
7. What is my marketing cost per contact?
8. How many new clients are necessary to reach my sales goal?

Evaluating the Completed Campaign
1. Did you reach your sales goal? Why or why not?
2. Did this campaign result in the sales of other products and/or services? Explain.
3. Were you able to stay within budget? Why or why not?
4. Provide a general description of the clients who bought the promoted product or service.
5. Did the marketing tools grab the attention of the target audience? Why or why not?
6. Is this target audience particularly profitable for my business? Why or why not?
7. How many hours did you personally dedicate to this marketing campaign? Did the marketing campaign consume too much time (keeping you from running your personal training business)?
8. Considering the amount of time you dedicated to running this campaign, would you consider hiring outside assistance (i.e., advertising agency)? Why or why not?
9. Identify three (3) things done well in this campaign. Explain.
10. Identify three (3) things to improve on for future deliveries of this campaign. Explain.

Figure 6-1: SMART Goals and Evaluating the Campaign

PART TWO:
SALES AND MARKETING STRATEGIES
(ON A BUDGET)

Okay ... let's be honest here. Before you bought this book you were aware of the following:

1. You knew very little about marketing.
2. Marketing is essential to growing your personal training business (i.e., increase sales, retain current clients).
3. Marketing requires an investment (i.e., time, effort and money).
4. You don't want to spend a lot of money on marketing.

It's true! Traditional marketing costs a lot more than most people would realistically spend. According to Ad Age (www.adage.com), this is what you would expect to pay for the following advertising opportunities:

- **$2.5 million** - cost to be displayed for four weeks on Times Square's biggest billboard
- **$1.55 million** - a 30 second commercial during the championship game of the 2015 NCAA Men's Division I Basketball Tournament
- **$750,000** - cost of a single "Brand Story" ad on Snapchat's Stories feed
- **$112,000** - average cost of 30 seconds of commercial time in prime time broadcast TV in 2014
- **$50,000** - cost of one full color ad on the front page of the New York Times

The budget for one advertisement, alone, is more than you might make in your entire career as a personal trainer! Luckily, you're not in an industry where this type of promotion is standard practice. The companies that resort to this type of high priced advertising are typically selling products (i.e., computers, cars, clothing, etc.), and they need to resort to "flashy" advertising to stay top of mind in a highly competitive global market. They hire an advertising agency to do all the work as they sit back and wait for the sales to come in.

Most personal trainers can't afford to pay an agency to do their marketing. For example, agencies can charge upwards of $300 per hour (which is not a realistic expense if you are only making $50 per hour with clients). The only other option is to do their marketing themselves.

This means personal trainers need to:
- Take time away from training clients to dedicate to marketing (i.e., planning, developing creative, implementation and evaluation).
- Get to know all forms of media (i.e., print, digital, etc.).
- Become proficient in communicating their message to potential clients (through various media)
- Be very creative.

Marketing doesn't come easy for most personal trainers. It requires a specific education and skill set that most personal trainers don't have. Regardless, with the right attitude and good information to guide you ... it can be done!

The next few chapters will discuss simple marketing strategies that personal trainers can implement to grow their business. In addition, Part Four of this book outlines sample marketing campaigns (including a wide variety of tactics and content for each) that you can review.

Chapter 7:
Grassroots Marketing

In any business, including personal training, marketing your products and services is essential to your success. Marketing is simply a way to let people know you have something they want or need. Unlike the mass marketing campaigns of large corporations and big box chains, grassroots marketing is a cost-effective marketing strategy that is a based on personal recommendations and a more local approach. Instead of using mass media forums (i.e., television and radio) to advertise their products, businesses rely on personal recommendations and word-of-mouth strategies within local communities to promote their products.

Why Grassroots Marketing Works

Because we have been bombarded over the years with media and advertisements on the television, in the subway, and on buildings and buses, people now generally ignore, avoid, or become oblivious to advertising techniques. This is also true for the Internet. If you look on any search page you will see Google ads, banner ads, and annoying "pop-ups" that are often dismissed or not paid attention to.

Over the years, people have learned to rely less on the messages manufactured by large companies and put more trust in independent sources. Information received by others has a layer of credibility because people generally believe others are speaking honestly and are unlikely to have an ulterior motive. Personal recommendations encourage others to try new products and services. If people are pleased with their purchase they will recommend it to others, producing a "ripple effect".

Grassroots Marketing Basics

At the heart of grassroots marketing is relationships. A business needs to build lasting relationships to grow a base of loyal customers who will promote their products and services. Instead of launching a marketing message that you hope appeals to many people, you target your efforts towards a small group. Your goal is to get the group to share your message with a much larger audience.

For example, the average number of friends a Facebook user has is 130 (according to StatisticBrain.com). If you have 20 active clients in your database, that represents an audience of 2,600 people who "may" hear about you and your business. If you play your cards right, and market your business the right way, your active clients may be the only people you need to target in order to grow your business effectively.

Grassroots marketing often uses unconventional or nontraditional methods, costs significantly less than more conventional marketing efforts, and can produce big results!

Targeting Your Efforts

The first step is to target people or groups that are influential to your business. The strategy is for them to use their influence to spread the word about you as a personal trainer to their friends, family, colleagues, and community. A personal trainer may choose to give one free fitness assessment and a personal training session to each of the doctors working at a local medical office in hopes they'll recommend their services to patients that could use the help. Another personal trainer may choose to give their clients t-shirts that say, "Feel Good Inside. Look Better Outside.". When friends and family members ask them about their shirt they will be proud to tell others about their experience with their personal trainer.

Grassroots Marketing Costs

In general, grassroots marketing will cost significantly less than a mass marketing campaign. Because these types of campaigns are "non-traditional" and more creative (primarily for budget purposes), they often feature low-cost and free campaigns, such as posting on social media or message boards, holding giveaways and contests, and other low-cost (but high impact) campaigns. Rather than take out expensive print advertising to reach a broad audience, grassroots marketers can afford to launch several smaller-scale campaigns to reach separate defined audiences.

Examples of Grassroots Marketing Campaigns

Grassroots marketing is all about spreading the word about your business and making sure the target audience hears the message loud and clear. Below are examples of low-cost grassroots marketing campaigns to increase exposure for personal trainers:

- Broadcast communications
- Social media posts
- YouTube videos
- Special offers and giveaways

Broadcast Communications

As you grow your business, your contact list will also increase in size. Because the world has become more dependent on the Internet and "instant" communication, gathering email addresses will be essential to expanding your business.

When using an email service (i.e., Microsoft Outlook or Gmail), broadcast emails can save valuable time and money, when used correctly. You can create one single email and distribute it to a list of up to 100 contacts at one time. Key things to remember when developing a broadcast email campaign include:

- Use your own contact list (of people who will expect an email from you)
- Avoid using the words "free", "prize", "bonus", or too many exclamation marks and capital letters (to avoid SPAM)
- Limit the number of images or attachments
- Send the email using an address your contact list will recognize
- Ask recipients to "white list" your email address in advance (to

avoid SPAM)
- Maintain a regular mailing pattern (customers remember you when your communications are frequent but not too often that they ignore you)

These rules also apply to broadcast text (SMS) messaging.

Social Media Posts

Social media refers to the interactions between people in virtual communities and networks, where they are creating, sharing, and exchanging information and ideas. This includes blogs and microblogs (i.e., Twitter, Reddit), social networking sites (i.e., Facebook, Pinterest, Instagram), and content communities (i.e., YouTube, SlideShare). The best part about all of these outlets is that it accounts are free!

Posting to one (or more) of these vehicles can get your message across instantly and to a community of people who know you and want to hear from you. Posts could include:
- Release of the new group training schedule
- Monthly promotion
- New client testimonial
- Announcing new contest or giveaway

YouTube Videos

If a picture is worth a thousand words, than a video must be worth a million! YouTube is the perfect example of how effective video can be, with more than one billion unique visitors per month watching and sharing videos they find on that site. Establishing a presence on YouTube is important for any business looking to grow.

Producing video to promote your business is easier than you may think. It can be as simple as using a digital camcorder (under $150.00), or the high definition camera on your smartphone, to record information that gets the attention of your target audience. Examples include:
- Client testimonials

- Client "before and after" results
- Personal training highlight reel
- Group training program highlight reel
- Q&A with a personal trainer
- Mini commercial

Special Offers and Giveaways

Potential customers are constantly looking to find "value" in their purchases. If what they paid is perceived to be less than what a product or service is worth, they are more likely to buy. A special offer sets the dollar value of a product or service and reduces the price to entice someone to buy. For example:

> "Buy 10 personal training sessions, and receive two sessions at no additional cost (a value of $150)."

A giveaway is a type of marketing promotion where something is given away for free. Businesses often use giveaways to spread the word about their products and services, to make themselves more memorable in the eyes of their customers, or to get people to try something new in the hopes that they will continue  to buy. For example, a personal trainer could go to the local "Warrior Dash" event and give the top five finishing teams a free one hour fitness assessment.

Final Thoughts

Grassroots marketing is most effective if you can identify a specific group of people and appeal to their likes and dislikes. If you waste time marketing to groups who aren't interested in your product, or who have no influence with other groups, you are wasting your valuable time and effort. Be sure to develop a way to gauge the success of your grassroots campaigns to track the effectiveness of each campaign, identify the ones that work well and can be used again, and get rid of the ones that don't produce results.

Chapter 8:
Bringing Fitness to the People Through Community Outreach

Every human being on the planet needs to be physically active on a regular basis to live a long, healthy life. But, because most people don't possess the motivation or drive to get active without a little (actually, A LOT) of coaxing, this is exactly what a personal trainer needs to hear when they are running their own business! There is an obvious need for personal training services, but it may be difficult to get your name "top of mind" with so many other personal trainers out there fighting for the business.

If you're reading this book it's safe to say that you don't have the budget to put a billboard up in Times Square or have a wealthy relative who would be willing to pay for a television commercial during the Super Bowl. Although it would be nice to have these marketing opportunities, they certainly aren't necessary when it comes to ensuring your local community keeps you top of mind when they are looking for fitness advice or exercise supervision.

In a tight knit community, outreach campaigns and showcasing your personal brand at local establishments can effectively help you gain credibility and loyal clients!

What is "Outreach"?

Outreach is "an activity of providing services to populations who might not otherwise have access to those services at no cost to the recipients" (Wikipedia, 2015). A key component of outreach is that the services are brought to the community and the group providing the services are mobile (bringing the services to where the people in need are located). In addition, outreach has an educational role, in raising awareness about underlying issues and services that are available to overcome these challenges.

For example, many major cities organize outreach groups to bring food and warm clothing to the homeless during colder months of the year or bring toys to children in orphanages during the holidays. Outreach efforts are designed to improve the quality of life for community residents wherever they may be.

Although outreach has typically been associated with not-for-profit organizations, your personal training business can benefit from providing services free of charge to groups that could use your knowledge and expertise. These efforts could be used as part of a grassroots marketing campaign in your community.

Getting the Most Out of Your "Sweat Equity"
In a new personal training business, with a small advertising and marketing budget, your time and effort is often sacrificed to help save money. For example, instead of paying to run a newspaper ad promoting your business, you spend hours putting flyers on windshields in the Target and Costco parking lots hoping to drive people to your website and inquiring about your results-based programs.

Although distributing flyers can get the word out there ... it really can't demonstrate effectively who you are (which is essential for personal training success), the extent of what you know, or what you can do as a motivational expert or fitness leader. Since you're already willing to sacrifice your own time to build your business, you might as well choose activities that create the most growth for your business!

When it comes to one-on-one services, people will rarely choose a provider that hasn't earned their trust or respect (especially if they are asking for $50+ per hour). Trust (or respect) is seldom attained reading through a brochure or browsing through the pages of your website. One-on-one interaction (either in person or via phone or email) is the best way to create a connection, establish credibility and differentiate yourself from your competition. The unique experiences you have with people are not easily forgotten and they will set you apart from other personal trainers focused on using more traditional marketing strategies.

Designing a Community Outreach Campaign

A community outreach campaign, just like any marketing strategy, requires a solid, well-executed plan to be successful. It requires the following steps:

1. Identify a captive audience.
2. Choose the ideal location.
3. Create a participant experience that is positive, educational and memorable.
4. Provide handouts or branded materials.
5. Have a "follow up" strategy.

Identify a Captive Audience

Although most people can benefit from a quality fitness and exercise experience, not everyone will want to participate. Think about your local community and identify groups of people that would welcome a free fitness class or workshop.

Because people are more likely to try new things when they are surrounded by people they know and are comfortable with, target established communities of people who meet on a regular basis (and have the means to afford your personal training services). Examples include:

- Corporate head office
- Sports teams
- Running groups
- Bridal Fair or Women's Show
- Weight loss support group

Choose the Ideal Location

Once you've identified your participant group, you need to secure a location that will work best to showcase your personal training talents in a group environment. Ideally, this location:

- Is easily accessible by the target audience.
- Requires little to no cost (i.e., public park, classroom, on site gymnasium, parking lot).
- Provides enough room for all participants.
- Is clean and safe.

<u>Create a Positive Participant Experience</u>
The goal of any outreach campaign is to provide participants with an experience that is both positive and memorable. Typically, an open event will include an audience that includes everyone from fitness "newbies" to workout "veterans". So, regardless of the level of fitness, you want everyone feeling good about their fitness experience and to motivate them to do it again! Ideally, your first experience with them establishes rapport, leaves a lasting impression and keeps you top of mind for anything (and everything) to do with fitness and wellness.

<u>Provide Handouts or Branded Materials</u>
The ultimate goal of any outreach campaign is to introduce your business to new potential clients and for them to consider you as their next personal trainer. Handouts (for an educational workshop) or branded materials (i.e., business cards, brochures or branded gear) provide them with valuable information that keeps you top of mind and ensures they can get in contact with you quickly and easily.

Final Thoughts
Personal training, as a business, is about relationships and interactions with clients and potential clients. Rather than investing a lot of money into traditional handouts, mailers and flyers (which can't demonstrate the actual experience of training with you) consider outreach campaigns in your community. This will give you an opportunity to showcase your expertise and differentiate you from your competitors.

Your time is your time is valuable. It's time to work "smarter", not "harder".

Chapter 9:
Your Website = Your Best Salesperson

Personal trainers are experts in exercise, fitness instruction and program design. They will spend hundreds of hours each year working with people, one-on-one, to help them achieve their health and fitness goals. They have mastered the art of motivation and are continuously reminding their clients that the effort they put in translates to the results they will achieve. Personal trainers live in a physical world where pushing, pulling, lifting and sweating are the norm. They know how to build muscles ... not websites.

Unless a personal trainer had previously worked in Information Technology (IT), the Internet (i.e., how it works, the rules of engagement, global statistics, etc.), how search engines work (i.e., Google, Yahoo, Live Search, etc.), and how to effectively build a highly searched website is something most have no clue about. And, much like someone walking into a gym for the very first time ... a personal trainer trying to figure out their own website can be a scary!

This chapter is not going to teach you how to design and code your own website (because that should be left to the experts). It is going to provide information about the importance of having a well designed and optimized site for your personal training business.

Websites 101

A website is a single domain (i.e., www.activPT.com) that consists of one or more web pages. More specifically, a website is hosted on a web server (which is used to store, process and deliver web pages to clients) and is accessible via the world wide web through an Internet address, or uniform resource locator (URL).

As of September 2015, there are just under 1 billion websites on the world wide web (including at least 4.74 billion web pages). Surprisingly, only a fraction of established businesses actually have a dedicated website!

If you have a personal training business and don't have a website, you are losing out on countless opportunities to grow your business. A well thought out and strategically planned website can be your best salesperson and marketing hub.

Why a Website is Important for Your Personal Training Business

In Chapter 2, you identified your target market. You know the characteristics and traits you are looking for in a potential client but going through the phone book and randomly calling people to introduce yourself isn't the most effective use of your time.

The same is true for the individual looking for a solution to their health and wellness problem. They typically know what they are looking for but they won't likely make the effort to call all the personal trainers in the phone book to find the right one. As well, they are most likely researching this information during the hours most personal trainers aren't answering their phones or booking appointments.

Although the phone book is a reliable resource for finding people and businesses, the Internet is now the place most people go to for information when they are curious about something or someone. The Internet is also interactive and delivers information to the user, providing qualified answers in seconds rather than spending hours using more traditional means.

So ... if your business doesn't have a website the majority of people who are looking for a personal trainer to help them with their specific fitness and exercise goals will NEVER find you.

Aside from being included in the 20.3 billion searches conducted each month by Americans alone (comScore.com, 2011), there are several other ways a website can significantly benefit your personal training business, including:

- Cost effective marketing
- Accessibility 24/7 (365 days a year)
- Convenience
- Credibility

Cost Effective Marketing

One of the most expensive upfront costs for any personal training business (aside from equipment and/or fitness accessories) is marketing and promotion. This includes the cost of high-quality color printing of branded materials (i.e., business cards , brochures, handouts, apparel and gear), which may be a few hundred to thousands of dollars. In addition, as you update or change these materials that increases your marketing costs over time.

A website, on the other hand, is essentially a digital branding tool. It represents your brand to the world visually (through text, images and video) and audibly (through podcasts and video with sound). A website can be easily updated and changed at any time. Visitors will always get the most current information whenever they visit your site.

If a client (or potential client) is looking for a brochure or other promotional materials, you can have them available for download on your site, saving you from reprinting costs (if there are updates and changes) and postage. This could equate to a savings of thousands of dollars a year!

Accessible 24/7 (365 days a year)

The Internet is "open for business" around the clock. This means your website and all social media accounts are accessible by whomever is looking for you 24/7, 365 days a year. Although you aren't physically training clients (or waiting by your phone) all hours of the day and night, your website can be your best sales person, marketing tool and assistant for scheduling appointments!

For example, at 11 o'clock at night a woman may be searching online for a personal trainer to help them lose weight in time for their summer wedding. They notice a friend shared one of your posts on Facebook and they find your Facebook page. Intrigued by the information and images on your page they click the link to view your website. When they get to your website they download your personal training brochure and find information on the "Bridal Bootcamp" starting in two weeks. They also submit their email address to receive your monthly eNewsletter and log into MindBody (your online scheduling software) to book their free fitness consultation on Friday afternoon at 3 o'clock. This all happened while you were at home watching Netflix.

Convenience
A well-designed (and functional) website makes the exchange of information easier and more meaningful for the end user. For example:
- A potential client can learn more about personal training without having to contact them, schedule an appointment or make a phone call.
- A potential client may be shy and is easily intimidated. They feel more comfortable researching information in advance before getting in contact with a potential trainer (via email or phone).
- An existing client can access articles, resources and/or workouts from the website (rather than having to carry around extra papers during their training session).
- An existing client can book their sessions online without having to call the trainer to coordinate over the phone (or email).

An effective website design also makes it easier for personal trainers to:
- Keep the most up-to-date information available online (without having to waste time and money reprinting new brochures, etc.)
- Gather contact information from qualified leads who are ready to buy personal training (via an opt-in form or subscription to an eNewsletter)
- Post their schedule and availability so clients can proactively schedule their sessions (instead of the countless phone calls

confirming, cancelling and rescheduling appointments)

<u>Credibility</u>
Personal training is a significant investment for most people. It not only takes a significant amount of time and multiple sessions to get results, there needs to be a great deal of trust with the personal trainer as well.

Before a potential client even considers contacting a personal trainer, they need to know that the candidate is knowledgeable, easy to get along with and is the "real deal". Most people will search the Internet to ensure they are buying from someone they can trust.

By having a well-designed and functional website you ensure potential clients know everything they need to about you (and the experience of training with you) through:
- Written content and blog posts
- Images that showcase your and your clients
- Testimonials from your clients (and peers)
- Downloadable brochures and resources
- Links to your social media accounts

When a personal trainer provides good service, positive word-of-mouth about their personal training business is likely to spread (especially via social media). Their website should be there to validate the "rumors" about them and their business when they physically can't. On the flip side, if negative press gets out there (whether it's valid or not), their website should be there to defend them and their business.

Regardless, the website speaks to the quality, character and credibility of the personal training business. It's your offense to market and establish your brand, and your defence when it comes to negative press or competitors invading your territory.

The Bottom Line
Unlike twenty years ago, before the Internet played such an essential role in our everyday lives, it is now critical for every business to have a website. More importantly, a business needs to have a website that is more than just a domain name (URL) put together with a "do-it-yourself"

service like Wix or Weebly. Your website needs to:

- Properly represent your brand
- Provide a solution to the problem(s) of your website visitor
- Be easy to navigate so visitors can find answers right away (regardless of what reason they have for being on your website)
- Be your best salesperson (24 hours a day, 7 days a week, 365 days a year)

A website should work for your business all hours of the day and night, converting web visitors to inbound emails and calls from qualified leads. But this requires more than just a pretty site. You need to maintain a website like you do your car. Your vehicle is meant to get you from point A to point B ... but requires a running engine, a destination and gas in the tank. Your website requires ongoing maintenance and needs to have a "heartbeat" to remain relevant in the eyes of search engines.

Because the Internet is such a powerful platform for personal trainers to leverage in growing their business, the next few chapters will go into more detail about search engines (i.e., Google), how to gain authority on the Internet, strategies for building out an effective website and how to leverage social media.

PART THREE:
The Power of Digital Marketing

Because it's been around for such a long time, we have become accustomed to traditional marketing. We still watch television, read magazines and listen to the radio on the commute to and from work. But, over the last decade, there has been a significant shift from traditional marketing (i.e., television, radio, newspaper and magazines) to more effective digital platforms. This is because digital marketing has evened the player field and can cater to the needs of both the advertiser and consumer. In a technologically driven society, where consumers are looking for information, instant feedback, control, convenience and value, marketing strategies needed to evolve to meet these needs! For example:

- Why would someone coordinate their schedule to be at home to watch their favorite television show when they could digitally record it and view it (without all the annoying commercials) at any time, day or night?
- Why would someone spend $9.95 for a printed copy of a fashion magazine at the newsstand down the street when they could access the complete edition online for FREE, including exclusive articles and real-time contests?

Granted, there are some people (myself included) that enjoy watching a show when it first airs on TV, actually flipping the pages of a captivating book and the slippery feel of a newly printed magazine. But, increasingly more people are wanting information and entertainment that suits their busy lifestyles and their pocketbook.

For business owners, digital marketing is also becoming the preferred form of advertising and promotions. Unlike traditional marketing (which sends information out to an intended audience), it is interactive and uses "two-way communication", where the audience can receive and then respond. This type of marketing captures the attention of bigger audience and keeps them engaged for longer periods of time. Here are some interesting facts to consider:

- Every month there are more than 10.3 billion Google searches, with 78 percent of U.S. Internet users researching products and services online. *(source: CMOCouncil.org)*
- Companies spent, on average, 25 percent of total marketing budgets on digital in 2014. *(source: Business2Community.com)*
- 80 percent of consumers do online research for major purchase decisions (and 46 percent count on social media when making such choices). *(source: Business2Community.com)*
- Content marketing (in 2015) generates 3 times as many leads as traditional outbound marketing, but costs 62 percent less. *(source: Hubspot.com)*

From a business perspective, there are several advantages to including digital marketing into your overall marketing plan (as a complement to your traditional marketing efforts):

- Level playing field
- Reduced cost
- Ability to measure (and evaluate)
- Not intrusive
- Greater exposure
- Greater engagement

Level Playing Field
Any business, no matter how small, can compete with a solid digital marketing strategy. Traditionally, a small personal training studio would have a hard time matching the prestige (and budget) of a large fitness club or recreation center. Online, a well thought out website that clearly

demonstrates your expertise and your focus on quality and customer service will keep your business top of mind. For example, some of the biggest fitness chains have some of the worst (an non user-friendly) websites.

Reduced Cost

Any small business (personal training or otherwise) can develop an online marketing strategy for very little cost and, potentially, replace the cost of expensive advertising (including Yellow Pages, print ads or radio).

Ability to Measure

Traditional marketing is hard to measure. As an example, you can pay for 10,000 direct mail pieces to be sent out to a specific area of the city but you have no measure of how many were noticed, read or who is interested. You just hope someone calls you and books a consultation. With digital marketing, you can see in real time what is (or is not) working and can adapt very quickly to improve your results. For example:

- Google Analytics can be used to measure specific goals you want to achieve for your personal training website
- MailChimp (an online email marketing service) can provide insight on how many people are opening, reading and clicking on links embedded in your emails

Not Intrusive

I'm fairly confident we all dislike receiving unsolicited calls or having door-to-door sales people ringing the doorbell. Online, people are protected from getting unwanted mail in their Inbox and can choose to opt out of any electronic communication. In fact, most inbound email comes as a result of the person opting in (i.e., providing their email address on a website) to receive the information they are interested in.

Greater Exposure

Your personal training business can be seen anywhere in the world from one single campaign (24 hours a day, 7 days a week, 365 days a year). This can be done for a fraction of the cost of a traditional campaign that had the same reach. In addition, a single campaign can last for far longer than a single direct mail piece or radio spot. A campaign you start today could still bring in business five years from now (if it is done right).

Greater Engagement

With strategic digital marketing, you can encourage your online audience to take action (via social media or email), click on the link to visit your website, read about your personal training services, conveniently buy them online and provide a review for other online visitors to see.

In addition, using social media share buttons on your website (or any other electronic communication) enables your message to be shared very quickly. For example, let's say you have 1,000 likes on your Facebook Business page. When you post to this page, everyone who has liked your page will see your post in their News Feed. Keep in mind that the majority of Facebook users have more than 200 friends, and that 12 percent of these friends actually see their "liked" posts. See the example below:

Facebook (Round 1) $= (1{,}000 \times 0.12) \times (200 \times 0.12)$
$= 120 \times 24$
$= 2{,}880$ views from the first of contact

Facebook (Round 2) $= (2{,}880 \times 0.12) \times (200 \times 0.12)$
$= 346 \times 24$
$= 8{,}304$ views from the second level of contact

Facebook (Round 3) $= (8{,}304 \times 0.12) \times (200 \times 0.12)$
$= 996 \times 24$
$= 23{,}904$ views from the third level of contact

Facebook (Round 4) $= (23{,}904 \times 0.12) \times (200 \times 0.12)$
$= 2{,}868 \times 24$
$= 68{,}832$ views from the fourth level of contact

Depending on how well the content is received, this level of engagement on Facebook (passed through four levels of contact) could literally happen in a matter of minutes! Just imagine what could happen in 24 hours, let alone a week or month! It's mind boggling!

What's even more astounding is the fact that the post didn't cost a single cent to post, yet had such a strong response. If you match the right message (including a sales promotion or tactic), at the right time, to the right audience with digital marketing, the return on investment goes through the roof!

As you can see, your message could spread to a large audience in a short amount of time (if the content if relevant, memorable, and intriguing) when it was endorsed by a trusted source online.

In the next few chapters you will learn more about online marketing, specifically as it relates to your personal training website (the primary platform for all your digital marketing strategies), and ways to plan for online marketing success!

Chapter 10:
Google, SEO and the Successful Personal Trainer

For new personal trainers, or personal trainers looking to grow their existing business, establishing a strong online presence is a "no brainer". Although the industry has typically used traditional sales and marketing strategies and tactics (i.e. posters, handouts, and advertised promotions), leveraging the power of search engines (i.e., Google) is essential to making the most of the business.

Personal Training – A Simple Business
There is a simple mindset when it comes to a personal training business. This is because of the simple fact that personal training is very "hands on" and requires little to no technology when compared to other service-based businesses (i.e. restaurant, retail store, or doctor's office). To be successful you need knowledge, experience, good communication skills, and a space to train your client. Free weights, cardio equipment, and other fitness accessories aren't necessary to challenge a client and produce measurable results, but they definitely add more to the services a personal trainer can offer.

Because personal training is such a "hands on" profession, trainers struggle to find the time to market themselves and generate new business. Most personal trainers work really hard to build a client base and then "hope" they don't ever leave. Unfortunately, that is not the best way to run a business.

Why Google?
The Internet has provided a brilliant way for personal trainers to market and advertise themselves (and their business) 24/7, 365 days a year. It's a marketing company that doesn't need to sleep, eat, or take bathroom breaks! Although the Internet has been available to most of us since the 1980's, Google has changed the way people around the world communicate with one another and how we stay connected.

Google, the most used search engine (and #1 website in the world), is reported to have over 65 percent market share of searches in the US (according to a recent Parse.ly Authority report reviewing Internet traffic for July 2013). If you want to get noticed on the Internet, and build your personal training business, you need to get to know the "rules" of Google!

Understanding Google Search
Google Search receives several hundred million queries each day. When a search term is put into the Google search bar, it searches through over 100 million gigabytes of data (3.6 billion pages – August 2013) to find the best possible answer to your request. At Google, they take their role in providing useful and impartial web results very seriously.

Google writes programs and formulas (also known as "algorithms") to deliver the best possible results each time. These formulas are constantly being improved to ensure the best results come up and that websites don't "game the system" to show up higher than those who truly deserve recognition. For example, Google ranks results based on over 200 different factors.

Search Engine Authority
The ultimate goal of web search engines (i.e., Google, Yahoo! Search, Live Search, etc.) is to effectively and efficiently connect people with the information they are searching for ... the moment they hit the "Search" button. When someone goes to Google, and puts search terms into the search bar, they expect the answer to their query at the top of page one (or at least the first 2 or 3 links). If they have to click through 6 or

7 of the links (or scroll through 2 or 3 pages or results) to get what they are looking for, they will most likely go to Yahoo! Search for a better response.

Just like your business competes against other businesses for customers, search engines must also compete for users. The search engine that does the best job of connecting people with the answers they are looking for, quickly and efficiently, will be used more often. In order to ensure search engines "get the job done right" they need to filter through all the information available on the Internet and rank domains (and web pages associated with these domains) based on its "authority" on a particular topic.

Therefore, the goal of any website is to gain authority so that it is treated favorably by search engines. Proving authority and credibility on a particular topic is critical for any website because it triggers a "domino effect":

1. The higher the website (via individual pages) will rank when using search engines.
2. The higher the website (via individual pages) ranks on a search engine results page, the more traffic you can expect to the sites pages.
3. The more traffic your website receives, the more likely the content presented on the pages are being read (and potentially shared with their social network).
4. The more your content is being read (and the more time people spend browsing through your website) the more likely anything that is promoted or sold on your site is seen by potential buyers.
5. The more potential buyers that visit your site, the more physical sales you can generate on your website
6. The more potential buyers that visit your site (and physical sales you generate), the more valuable your site becomes to vendors who also want to market to the visitors that frequent your website.

Establishing website authority takes time, effort and a well though out strategy. It requires a well-designed website framework, the consistent development of well-written "unique content" (that shows authority in a specific topic area) and an ongoing digital marketing strategy!

Search Engine Optimization (SEO)

Search Engine Optimization (SEO) is the culmination of activities that seeks to generate productive "organic" traffic (unpaid search engine results) from search engines (i.e. Google, Yahoo! Search, Live Search, etc.). Although SEO, prior to 2012, was associated with marketing scams and unethical business practices, the rules of the game have now changed and SEO has become essential to business success on the Internet.

Regardless of the search engine you choose to use, there are three primary factors that have the most effect on a website or web page's SEO:

1. Keywords – Identifying the right keywords for your business.
2. Content – Produce great (and unique) content.
3. Links – Focus on building quality links pointing to your site.
4. Social Media – Get people to share your content on social media sites (i.e., Facebook, Twitter, Google+, Pinterest, Instagram, etc.).

The Bottom Line

The Internet, for small local businesses to large multibillion dollar global corporations, is the most powerful (yet misunderstood and underutilized) sales and marketing platform. As consumers, we only see the surface of what the Internet has to offer (i.e., the images and writing on the web page) ... the tip of the iceberg. Over the next few chapters, you will learn more about the "rules of the Internet", how to play by these rules, and leverage its power using strategies that will consistently reward you over time.

Chapter 11:
Why Content is (Still) King

Technology has changed the way businesses advertise. Unlike 20 years ago, when millions of people planned their schedules around the next episode of "Friends" or "Seinfeld" (and commercials effectively got their message across), traditional advertising has become less and less effective. The advent of the Digital Video Recorder (DVR) and streaming video services (i.e., Netflix, Hulu, Shomi, etc.) gave consumers the freedom to watch their favorite shows, at a time that was convenient for them, without all the annoying commercials.

Consumers are also paying less attention to advertisements in magazines and print media and have learned to ignore sidebar advertising on web pages, online banners and pop-up ads. They have become immune to obvious advertising and have become more selective to content that shows value to them. They don't want to be sold ... they want to be well educated.

For businesses looking for alternate ways to engage their potential customers (especially via the Internet), content marketing became the preferred weapon in today's marketing battleground!

What is Content Marketing?
Unlike traditional advertising, content marketing is defined as:

"A strategic marketing approach focused on creating and distributing valuable, relevant, and consistent content to attract and retain a clearly-defined audience - and ultimately, to drive profitable consumer action."

In a nutshell, content marketing is the art of communicating with your customers and prospects without actually selling. Instead of pitching your products or services, you are delivering information that makes your buyer more intelligent. The essence of this content strategy is the belief that if we, as a personal training business, deliver consistent, ongoing valuable information to potential clients, they will ultimately reward us with their business and loyalty.

Quality Content Should Be Focused on the Customer
So ... when it comes to digital marketing, you may have heard that "Content is King". Well, of the 200+ factors that search engines analyze when ranking websites ... written content is still at the top of the list!

This should come as no surprise because (as outlined in Chapter 8):
1. The main goal of any search engine is to connect end users with the best content possible.
2. If an end user is satisfied with how a search engine connected them to the information they were looking for (i.e., fast, effective, efficient, relevant, etc.) they will continue to use that particular search engine.
3. If your content is valuable to the end user, who is seeking answers to a specific question (and they have a good experience), they are more likely to come back.
4. In addition, if a search engine can generate more loyal users (and gain market share) because they do a good job of connecting end users to the information they are looking for, they are more appealing to advertisers who are willing to pay for the eyes of the search engine's users.

In the end, the customer experience is what determines how they perceive a brand and how they ultimately "feel" about it. So, when writing content you should be more focused on creating a good customer experience versus just writing content for content's sake.

When writing quality content you should be focused on genuinely communicating with your customers. This means actually listening to what they have to say, addressing their concerns and making them happy. By putting the needs of your customers first:

- The content you write will better fit the needs of your website visitors.
- You will better engage your current visitors.
- You will create a better customer experience, producing more advocates of your brand, and increase positive customer reviews.

Creating quality content focused on the customer experience is all about meeting customers where they are and then walking them on a journey towards trust, loyalty and an eventual purchase.

There are four (4) stages anyone, regardless of what they are searching for, will go through before they make a purchase:

Awareness

This is the very first step on any customer's journey and is typically when they are most likely using informational searches to educate themselves before they buy. They are researching products and services that help them overcome a problem they are trying to resolve. These visitors are more interested in reading content that helps them explore (in a non-threatening way) the topic they are interested in learning about.

Interest

When people move into this stage, they make a transition from informational searches to navigational queries. At this point they have interacted with your brand enough times (i.e., website, downloads, social media, etc.) that you have made it past the "first round". Now they are interested in sorting through the finer details between your brand and your competitors, and what makes your company worthwhile pursuing.

Content that positions your company as innovative and a thought leader, someone they can trust when they want help solving a problem they are facing.

Desire

When people move from the interest to the desire stage, they already have a good idea of which solution best fits their needs but they are not ready to complete their purchase. These customers are interested in learning more to help them make their final decision. They want to review content that guides them through their choices and helps them understand why your brand is truly worthy of their investment. They will use search engines to narrow down the options available and use websites to move from the desire to the action stage.

Action

People who are using search engines in the Action phase know exactly what they want to find so their queries are transactional. They want to find a page that makes it easy and painless to complete a transaction (i.e., purchase, book appointment, etc.).

Now that you understand the stages from awareness to purchase, review the recommendations below to best align your content with each phase of their journey:

- Identify keywords based upon each phase of a customer's journey (make sure the content addresses the specific purpose of each stage).
- See how your content relates to each phase and identify gaps (refer back to the keywords identified and see what keywords are not utilized through the phases and develop content that addresses the gaps).
- Optimize content for keywords
- Develop new content to fill gaps
- Use quality metrics to monitor progress:
  - Awareness: views of articles or videos
  - Interest: contest sign-ups or buyer guide views
  - Desire: competitive matrix or reviews
  - Action: online purchase or face-to-face sale

Final Thoughts

For personal trainers to succeed in online marketing, it's important to focus on creating an experience for their website visitors. That means writing content to that speaks to the needs of their potential customers at any stage of their buying process ... not just keywords on a page.

Chapter 12:
Keywords and Search Engine Authority

Regardless of the ever-changing landscape of the Internet, and the rules by which search engines rank websites, one thing has stayed pretty consistent from the start ... the effective use of keywords.

A keyword (or keyword phrase) is generally a word (or series of words) that represents a topic of importance. On the Internet, people use keywords as a way to put into words a topic in which they are searching for information. Keywords are essential to any successful website because:

- Keywords are the foundation of all your website content. Every page on your website should tie back to a keyword or keyword phrase that is relevant to your business.
- Keywords help visitors understand the purpose of your page. A visitor will often scan for keywords they searched for when reading the content of a page to ensure the website is relevant and useful.
- Keywords help search engines understand the purpose of your page. When a search engine "crawls" your website pages to index them it will look at the keywords on the page to determine the purpose of your pages (and your authority in providing answers to associated questions).

Keyword Research

Keyword research is a practice used to find and research actual search terms people enter into the search engines when conducting a search. This is typically done by a search engine optimization professional but can also be done on your own using online tools (i.e., Google Keyword Tool, SEMrush.com, or Google Adwords: Keyword Planner). Keyword research is done in an effort to achieve better rankings for your web pages in search engines.

Different Types of Keywords

There are two categories of keywords: broad keywords and long-tail keywords. Broad keywords are single words or short phrases that, while they apply to your industry and/or business, they might also apply to every other business in your industry (or even other industries). Long-tail keywords tend to be longer phrases that are more specific to your business or industry.

Broad keywords are essentially general to your business, incur a high search volume and face a lot of competition. These keywords are difficult to rank for and get traffic. The visitors from these keywords are less likely to become qualified leads.

On the other hand, long-tail keywords are specific to your business, are searched less often and face little competition. As you can imagine, these are easy to rank and get traffic for and visitors who search these keywords are more likely to become leads because they are more specific in what they are searching for.

In the beginning, it's best to start by targeting long-tail keywords because they are much easier to rank for and they bring the most relevant and qualified traffic looking for your area of expertise.

Choosing the Right Keywords

When you first start brainstorming keywords, it can be difficult to identify the right words to associate with searching for your authority website. Whether you are writing a blog for the first time or have been writing articles for years, ask yourself the following questions:

1. What are important (and relevant) topics based on your area of

authority?

2. What common questions do you think your website visitors would ask?

3. How would you describe your authority website to someone who has never heard of it?

<u>Important (and Relevant) Topics</u>

To begin, think of generic topics (or buckets) you want to rank for in search engines. These would be topics that are most often discussed by the target audience for your site. Generate a list with anywhere from five to ten topic buckets for your authority website. These topic buckets will then be used to focus more specific keywords down the road.

For example, if you are a strength and conditioning coach developing an authority website for elite level athletes, you might have the following general topic buckets:

- Strength training
- Cardiovascular training
- Power training
- Training programs
- Injury prevention and rehabilitation
- Performance testing
- Nutrition

Each topic bucket is different but generic in nature. There are a wide variety of subtopics that can be created within in each one.

<u>Common Questions by Web Visitors</u>

When it comes to developing a successful authority website, answering common questions posed by your target audience is a great way to produce quality content and show true authority to search engines. Remember, search engines are focused on matching the right web pages to the queries of searchers on the Internet. If your web page provides an authoritative response to the question ... you will rank higher in the search query.

Now that you have a list of generic topic buckets, it's time to identify keywords that fall into those buckets. These are keyword phrases you think are important to rank for in the search engine results pages (SERPs) based on the fact your target audience is most likely conducting searches for those specific terms.

Using the "strength training" topic bucket from above, some keyword phrases that people might submit for search could include:

- Strength training program for basketball
- Strength training for football
- Strength training exercises for women
- Strength training for rehabilitation
- What is strength training
- Is strength training safe for youth

Complete this task for each of your topic buckets. Keep in mind that this step isn't to come up with your final list of keyword phrases, it's simply a "brain dump" of phrases that you think might get searched. Down the road you will narrow down this list to help you focus your writing.

Describing Your Website

Your website visitors may not know all the industry keywords for the relevant topics you have in depth knowledge about. Instead, they will search using keywords they are familiar with. You want to think about the "elevator speech" used to explain your website to someone, with no prior knowledge of what you do, in just a few quick sentences. Using the example above, your description may include the following:

"ACTIVPT.com is a online information source for people interested in learning more about strength and conditioning for athletes who are serious about pursuing a career in sport. If you are looking for information on training programs, resources and tools that will give you an "athletic edge" this website is a great place to gather information and find the right strength and conditioning coach for your needs."

Also, keep in mind that keywords may be different in various parts of the world. For example, what is "pop" in one part of the world may be "soda" or "cola" in another.

Additional Tips

- Ensure the keywords you choose are what people are actually searching for. Put yourself in the shoes of a potential client who needs your services. Think about the words he/she would type into the search bar to find a business that does exactly what you do.
- Make sure your keywords are relevant to your content. Although keywords are used to search for web pages with helpful information, the content on your web pages need to reflect the initial query and be relevant to the topic searched.
- Your keywords are a part of your website branding strategy so be sure to use consistent language that references these keywords effectively and often. The last thing you want to do is confuse your web visitors with conflicting information.
- When coming up with your long-tail keywords be specific to areas of expertise and knowledge that differentiate you from other personal training authority websites. For example, instead of "strength and conditioning coach" you could use "certified strength and conditioning coach in Orange County".

Final Thoughts

Against popular belief, an effective website (with ample traffic and the ability to convert visitors to qualified buyers) doesn't just "happen". It requires a lot of thought and planning to develop the structure and framework for long term success. Take the time to carefully think about how your website will represent your business and take the steps towards building online respect and authority that will set the groundwork for the future.

Homework Assignment (Optional)

Using the information provided in this chapter, complete the "Keywords Worksheet" (Figure 9-1).

- DETERMINING YOUR KEYWORDS -

What are important (and relevant) topics based on your area of expertise as a fitness professional?

1. _____   6. _____
2. _____   7. _____
3. _____   8. _____
4. _____   9. _____
5. _____   10. _____

What are examples of broad keywords that pertain to your area of expertise as a fitness professional?

1. _____   6. _____
2. _____   7. _____
3. _____   8. _____
4. _____   9. _____
5. _____   10. _____

What are examples of long-tail keywords that pertain to your area of expertise as a fitness professional?

1. _____   6. _____
2. _____   7. _____
3. _____   8. _____
4. _____   9. _____
5. _____   10. _____

What common questions do you think your web visitors would ask?

1. _____
2. _____
3. _____
4. _____
5. _____

Figure 12-1: Keywords Worksheet

Chapter 13:
Writing (Your Own) Killer Content

Of all the chapters in the book, this may be the most frightening of them all (especially if you haven't written a blog post before). It's time to write content for your website.

Granted, you don't have to write the content for your site. You could spend the money and have someone else write content for you ... but I strongly urge you write for your own site in an effort to ensure the content and voice truly represents YOU (which is what your business is built around).

As a personal trainer, your knowledge and how you communicate with your clients is what truly differentiates you from your competitors. How you speak, your tone of voice and what you say encompass a training experience with you. Because your website may be someone's first introduction to you ... it should genuinely represent an interaction with you as well.

If you haven't written a blog post before, have very little experience or have not been taught now to write an effective blog post, this section will prove to be incredibly important (and you may want to reference this from time-to-time).

Getting Started

The hardest part about writing is getting started. Writing a piece of work is just like baking a cake. You need a recipe, the right ingredients, the oven at the right temperature and letting it bake for the right amount of time before it's done. A good blog post requires the following "ingredients":

- Topic
- Title
- Opening line
- Purpose
- Call to action

Topic

Choosing the right topic to write about on your blog is crucial if you want to engage your readers. Rushing the choice of topic can set you off in the wrong direction and can, often times, end up being a complete waste of time and effort.

Although there is the odd time that an idea for a post hits you right away, most times you can expect a post idea to require some cultivating before it's just right. Below are some ideas to help you identify potential topics and get them ready for writing:

1. Get a blank notebook and put a single idea at the top of each page. Make sure each topic is different from the rest. Choose topics that matter to you, that matter to your target demographic, or both.
2. Set aside time each day to scan through each page to see if a topic "connects" with you. You need to be inspired to write good content.
3. When you "connect" to an idea start to brainstorm valuable points that you can write about (think about reader needs that your post can help them overcome).
4. Once a particular idea has enough direction and focus, you are ready to start writing.
5. Don't rush this process. Let it happen naturally and organically. Not only will you enjoy the process more, you will also end up with a better piece of writing!

Title

Titles are incredibly important for getting people to your website, let alone reading your blog post, and these words can be the difference between a blog post getting noticed (and spreading like wildfire in social media circles and the Internet) or being a beautifully written piece of work that never gets read.

Blog post titles are incredibly important because they dictate whether a reader will choose you over another option. It needs to grab their attention and show them you are going to answer their question better than the other search results. They are the most powerful words that you write.

The blog post title should include the following (at least one, if not more):

- **Keywords** - to grab the attention of the readers looking for specific content and for SEO purposes.
- **Power Words** - words that evoke an emotional response right away (i.e., FREE, secrets, stunning, easy, stunning, etc.)
- **Benefit** (at least one) - the reader needs to know that if they take the time to read your post, it will benefit them
- **Controversy, Strong Opinion or Debate** - controversy is one of the those things that just tends to pique people's interest (but you will also attract strong reactions in people that you need to be prepared for)
- **Asking a Question** - People who respond to these types of posts are more likely to respond and leave comments (especially if the title directs questions at the reader)
- **Humor** - this can be tricky (if a joke falls flat) but can be effective in making posts go viral

In addition, blog titles should be short, to the point, and concise. This is also beneficial for SEO purposes.

The Body of the Post

First, and foremost, any blog post should have a reason for being. You should be asking yourself the following questions:

- What's the point of the post?

- What am I trying to communicate?
- What impact do I want to have on my reader?
- How will this information benefit my reader?
- So what?!!?

All the planning that you've done in advance will go to waste if your blog post has no real point to the reader. If you want your writing to be more than just something for them to read to "kill time" you need to focus your writing to "matter" to you and them.

In order to do this, and stay focused throughout the writing process, it's important to have a goal to achieve with the post before you write it (i.e., to help the reader properly perform a push-up, to demonstrate how to set up a TRX Suspension Trainer, etc.). It's important to refer back to this goal when you are not sure if the writing is on track.

Adding Depth

Once you've completed writing your blog post, and you are happy with the flow of the information from beginning to end (achieving the goal you set out at the beginning of the writing process) it's important to go back through it and add more depth.

Adding depth refers to making the blog post even more useful and easier to understand. There are several techniques you can use to provide a richer reader experience including:

- *Using Examples* - relate the information you are sharing into real life application
- *Adding an Analogy or Story* - real life stories help people relate to the content even more effectively as it puts a face and a name to someone looking for a solution to a problem (just like the reader)
- *Adding Your Opinion* - if you're writing about something in the news (i.e., a controversial topic) provide your own perspective to the story, over and above reporting the facts
- *Adding Quotes* - adding the voice of another person who validates your writing is effective in creating credibility (i.e., quote someone talking about your topic or something unrelated, but still relevant to the topic)

- **Suggested Articles to Read** - include links to other articles that are helpful for the reader to get a more well-rounded answer to their problem or query
- **Adding Illustrations, Charts or Infographics** - include images, charts or visuals that help to better explain the concepts (because pictures are sometimes worth a thousand words)

The more you add to the reader experience, the more likely they will read other blog posts and become an advocate of your brand. The richer the reader experience, the faster you can build the traffic to your site.

Length

According to Medium.com, the optimum length of a blog post takes a reader 7 minutes to complete. That equates to approximately 1,600 words. Keep in mind there is a direct proportion to the number of images you may add to the post and the number of words then required. The more images you include the fewer words are required to fill the 7 minutes of reading content.

With that being said, this is using statistical data from thousands of large websites tracking all aspects of their online marketing campaign. For your business, as a personal trainer or growing fitness business, it is more important to write shorter articles more consistently (i.e., 300 to 750 words, once a week) than to dedicate hours of your time trying to churn out a single 1,600 word blog post.

Adding the Finishing Touches

Although the writing is critical to the success of your authority website, there are ways to add more value to each blog post you write. To add more "star power" to your posts and differentiate them from your competitors, consider the following:

- **Add Images** - this creates a visual experience that breaks up the monotony of words on the screen
- **Add Charts and Diagrams** - charts and diagrams reinforce more complex information so the user understands the concepts more concretely
- **Use Sub Headings** - sub headings break up complex concepts

into smaller chunks, that make it easier to understand and hold the reader's attention

- *Use Short Paragraphs* - long paragraphs tend to lose readers (keep paragraphs to under five sentences)
- *Break Large Posts Up Into Multiple Posts* - if your content ends up being longer than 1,600 words, consider breaking it up into multiple posts (or a series), to get more bang for your content
- *Highlight and Reinforce Main Points* - highlight, bold or use colors to reinforce main points in your content

Quality Control

After you've put so much time and effort into the writing of your post, it's important to ensure the quality of your writing is ready to publish. Take the time to READ YOUR POST OUT LOUD to ensure it flows properly and is withing the 7 minute window for length. This also gives you an opportunity to check the post for spelling errors and improper grammar. If you are not particularly good with checking grammar make sure you have someone else available to check this for you. This is critical to how your readers perceive you and the quality of information you have to provide.

This is the last step (and most important step) before hitting "Publish" and making your blog post live on your website. This will immediately differentiate you from the majority of blog posts that do not check for language quality.

Frequency

A good place to start is to publish a blog post at least once every 7 days. This is the industry standard for most serious blog sites. It shows both search engines and your readers that you have a lot of knowledge to share and that you want to add value to the Internet.

Ideally, daily posts are what search engines are looking for but that is highly unlikely if you are a single-author publisher. Instead, focus on putting out quality content at a pace that works for you. As you get more proficient with writing your content you can get more out in a faster time line.

Types of Blog Posts

We are all creatures of habit, and this also translates to what and how we write. We tend to stick to topics that are comfortable and writing information in the same style. Unfortunately, that does not make for a complete website with information that is intriguing or that will bring readers back time and time again.

If you're having a hard time writing something that inspires you or are looking to change things up for your readers, here are 10 different types of blog posts you may want to consider:

1. Checklists and To-Do's
2. Guest Posts
3. How-To's and Tutorials (Video)
4. Infographics
5. Interviews
6. Lists
7. Podcast (including show notes)
8. Resource List (including links to URLs)
9. Reviews
10. Videos

Checklists and To-Do's

If someone is looking to cook something they've never made before they go to a recipe for step-by-step instructions on how to do it right. When someone has a question, and search for answers online, they are looking for straight answers or at least information that leads them in the right direction. Although this is somewhat similar to a "How To", these posts tend to focus on how to do something very efficiently and lists out the actual steps to take ... to make sure nothing is forgotten.

Guest Posts

One great way to take the pressure off of writing on your own authority website is to get guest writers to contribute content that speaks to their expertise. The motivation for a guest writer is to drive traffic from your website to theirs. But ... you can also leverage the audience of the contributing writer as they will promote this article to their website (and social media) as well.

Not only do you get a break from writing, you can leverage the audience of the contributing writer by having them follow the article to your website. Regardless, it's important that you still oversee and review all content before you publish it on your site, to ensure good quality writing and content that appeals to your target audience.

How To's and Video Tutorials

The reason why many people type words into a search bar is because they want to get "something" done ... but aren't sure how to get started (i.e., deadlift, chin up, kettle bell swings, etc.). So, one of the most effective ways to produce writing that is valuable to your website visitors is to create posts that clearly and effectively explain "how to" do something.

Although there is the hesitation to share expertise and knowledge on exactly how to complete a task (because that may take away business from someone who may actually pay you to do the work for them) a 350 to 500 word article or three minute video tutorial will not give away all of your business secrets. If anything, it's viewed by your readers as a contribution to your online community.

Lists

Lists are a great way to organize and streamline information into a numbered list, making it easy for readers to understand and put into action. They are effective because they put together valuable information in a way that is easy and efficient to read and comprehend. Examples include:

- 5 Exercises to Help Reduce Low Back Pain
- Top 10 Exercise DVDs under $20
- 8 Essentials to Include in Your Gym Bag
- 7 Ways to Avoid the Holiday Bulge this Season

Infographics

An infographic is a graphical representation of information on a particular subject that can help simplify concepts and/or create a more captivating experience. Ideally, an infographic should be visually engaging and contain subject matter that is appealing to your target audience. In short, infographics are a great way to engage your readers, especially those who do NOT have the patience to read a screen full or words.

You can find infographics on a wide variety of topics on the Internet. When you find one that speaks to a topic that you feel is appropriate for your readers you can simply write a review article on it and expand on the information it shares. This also gives you an opportunity to backlink to the website where it is originally found.

Interviews

If you're having a tough time coming up with copy (or just need a break) interviews are a great way to create unique content and venture into information that may be outside your comfort zone. You can either do a live podcast, video interview or written "question and answer" article. You can interview industry experts, real life customers or people in a different industry to get a fresh perspective. Interviews are especially useful if the guest also has their own website or blog. Once the post goes "live" you can have them backlink to your post for added benefit!

Podcasts and Show Notes

Podcasting is a form of audio broadcasting on the Internet. It's a powerful way to share your voice, your creativity and your thoughts with your audience. It is also a great way to build a passionate audience for your area of authority.

In addition to this, behind every great podcast are the show notes which can be published as a blog post. Podcasts and sound files can be transcribed using online services or software (prices vary), which are a cost effective tool versus manual transcription.

Resource List

Similar to a "list post", resource lists include links to content from other website pages from other websites (or other pages on your own site). Resource lists are perfect if you are just learning about a topic and have website pages that you used to gather valuable information. This gives you an opportunity to share your resources with your readers and also helps you build relationships with other websites (i.e., backlinking). Examples include:

- 10 Certification Organizations for New Personal Trainers
- Top 20 Pinterest Boards Exercise Motivation
- 50 Websites Every Personal Trainer Should Bookmark

Reviews

There are typically two types of reviews you can write: a single product review or a compare-and-contrast review. Regardless, you have a chance to highlight your expertise and knowledge in the area and can persuade someone who is looking to buy a product or service. People who are reading reviews are moving towards a final buying decision and are looking for expert advice.

Depending on the product or service you are reviewing, you may get free samples or product from companies wanting to be on your blog, offers to be a contributing writer or backlinks to their website. You can also use a review to include a resource list of websites that also provide additional perspective (or reviews) on the same product or service.

Videos

If you've already been creating videos and posting them on YouTube, you have content that is ready to use for your authority website! Videos are a great way to build rapport and differentiate yourself from your competitors. When you embed the video it also keeps your visitors on your web page for longer and adds more value to your written content.

How to Stay Motivated to Blog

When it comes to writing a new blog, the hardest part is staying motivated to write when your blog posts aren't getting noticed (at least not yet). One thing to keep in mind is that this is not a reflection of your writing. Typically, a website is put into the "sandbox" for a certain amount of time so it can be carefully monitored for activity and if it has the potential to add great value to the Internet. There is a lot of debate regarding domain age and ranking. We don't know exactly how much time is required before a website is out of the "sandbox" but we do know that younger websites have a more challenging time ranking than sites that have been around for longer (and that actively create quality content and generate backlinks to reputable sites).

The good news is that the hardest part of writing your blog is the initial launch phase. This is where you do a lot of writing, strategically market to get readers, approach contributing writers and get a system in place for the long term growth and development of your site. Once you get rolling, your site is full of content, and traffic and your blog community is growing, the day to day process gets easier and easier.

In the meantime, below are a few tips to help you stay motivated and on track to creating valuable and consistent website content:

- ***Identify the parts of the writing process you truly enjoy.*** Focus on the parts of the writing process that you really enjoy and look forward to. For example, you may not like researching but enjoy personal commentary. Identify the importance of research to make your personal commentary really intriguing and then dive into the writing once all the preparation is done!

- ***Establish writing habits (or a checklist).*** It takes time to establish habits that start to feel natural. Writing habits are different for everyone and can include:
  - When you write
  - Where you write
  - The process for creating an article (i.e., topic, speaking points, images, research, etc.)
  - The kinds of posts you write (i.e., interviews, comedy, controversy, top 10 lists, etc.)

- ***Find a new place/environment to work.*** Sometimes changing up "where" you write can reinvigorate the creative process. Go to a different room in the house, put a plant on your desk, play some inspiring music or go to your local library or a coffee shop. You'll be amazed how the smallest changes can make the biggest difference!

- ***Write a completely different kind of post.*** Most writers tend to favor one or two types of posts (i.e., research, review, top 10 lists, "how to" posts, controversial topics, etc.). To challenge your writing ability choose a type of post you don't typically choose. This will get you thinking differently about a topic and how to deliver it effectively to your audience.

- ***Get "constructive" feedback from people you trust.*** It's easy getting stuck in a writing "bubble" and not challenging (or improving) your writing style. Have a friend, family member or associate read through your work and provide feedback before you post. It's amazing what you miss when yours are the only eyes on your writing.

- *Put yourself in your audience's shoes.* Don't forget "who" you are writing the article for. It's easy to get caught up in writing for yourself versus for your target audience and what matters most to them (and what they want to learn).
- *Have someone else set your writing deadline.* When you are accountable only to yourself it can be difficult to stay on track with your writing. Set a deadline with someone who will also be reading (and critiquing) your work.
- *Have someone else read and edit your writing.* When you spend so much time writing it can get tough to read your own work and be completely objective. Find someone, whom you trust, to read and review your writing. This will provide good feedback and help you to continually improve your writing style.

The Bottom Line
Your website is the most powerful tool in your marketing arsenal. It acts as your best marketing tool and salesperson, 24 hours a day, 7 days a week and 365 days a year. It is a direct reflection of you, your knowledge and expertise, your personality and differentiates you from the competition.

Although the initial "look" and "design" are important, the delivery of quality content is crucial to getting new clients and keeping existing ones. The information shared need to be honest and real ... because a client will know the difference once they meet you in person.

By adding new content on a consistent basis your remain current and relevant in the eyes of your potential clients and search engines that connect you to a captive audience.

Homework Assignment (Optional)
Using the information provided in this chapter, complete the "Blog Post Outline Worksheet" (Figure 11-1).

- BLOG POST OUTLINE -

TOPIC	
KEYWORD FOCUS	
TITLE	
TYPE OF POST	☐ Checklist ☐ List ☐ Guest Post ☐ Podcast ☐ How-To ☐ Resource List ☐ Infographic ☐ Review ☐ Interview ☐ Video
IMAGE REQUIRED	☐ Yes ☐ No Description:
CHART OR DIAGRAM	☐ Yes ☐ No Description:
KEY POINTS TO COVER	1. 2. 3. 4.
REFERENCES	1. 2.
DEADLINE	

Figure 13-1: Blog Post Outline Worksheet

Chapter 14:
Building Online Trust, Reputation and Authority

The primary function of marketing is to increase sales for your business. In a service based business, like personal training, relationships are the number one key to success. If this is the case, then trust is the foundation of any sale. If you ask any of the most successful sales organizations in the world, they will tell you that building trust is vital in their dealings with customers.

Building trust isn't something that happens in an instant, it's something that takes time. Forming strong relationships and ensuring long-term success with your personal training clients (and people they refer to you) involves establishing T.R.U.S.T.:
1. Truth - From your client's point of view, lying is the number one way to lose their trust and business forever.
2. Reliability - This is where the foundation of trust is built. Every time you make a promise to your client, and deliver on that promise, you earn their trust. It's about being there for your client before, during and after the sale.
3. Understanding - When you invest the time to understand your client's needs, you are building their trust by making the effort to see the world through their eyes. Understanding not only builds trust, it also gives you the confidence and tools to provide them with the right solution.

4. <u>Service</u> - There's no better way to build and maintain your client's trust than by providing them with ongoing personalized service and support. To stay on top of the activities essential for sales success, ask yourself these questions:

5. <u>Time</u> - Building trust does not happen overnight. It's the culmination of everything you do over time (big and small) that helps you build lasting relationships.

Building trust can take weeks, months or even years to accomplish. Although this works in a face-to-face scenario, the Internet is a completely different "animal". Website visitors searching for a personal trainer online aren't going to be as patient!

In fact, users often leave web pages in 10 to 20 seconds if they don't find what they are looking for. Pages with a clear value proposition can hold someone's attention for much longer, but that is not the case in most instances.

People use the Internet to access information quickly and efficiently. They want a quick answer and don't have time to waste on anything else. Because of this fact, people typically have time to read only a quarter of the text on a web page that gets their attention (which means pages they don't like are read even less).

How to Build Trust on the Internet
You're probably wondering how useful a website really is for your business, especially if active visitors stay for less than a minute. You're regretting all the time and money you may have spent trying to get your existing website ranked on Google (because someone said you should). Based on what you just read, all that work was wasted because it takes time to earn the trust of a new personal training client (i.e., phone calls and face-to-face meetings). A 20 second visit to your website is hardly enough time to build that kind of trust.

You would be mistaken.

If a first time web visitor likes your site, the probability of them returning to your site again, or viewing more content within your site, is extremely high. Actually, it's a lot like online dating. If a person sees a profile that interests them, they will bookmark it and return when they are comparing that person to other possible candidates. This person is doing their homework to find out if there is the potential for a long term, mutually beneficial relationship.

Now, take a step back and think about your potential client. You can assume they are:
1. Unhappy with at least one aspect of their health or physical appearance
2. Not comfortable seeking out the help of a stranger
3. Cautious about moving forward because they don't want to choose the wrong personal trainer (i.e., over promise and under deliver, no "working" chemistry, etc.)

Someone looking for the right personal trainer will most likely research potential candidates before they reach out and make contact. The Internet is a wealth of information that can be accessed by anyone, at any time, while remaining completely anonymous. This provides the perfect resource for people looking to find a personal trainer they can relate to and believe they can trust.

With that in mind, think about your website as your "personal trainer profile" on the Internet. Your website gives you a chance to:
1. Your philosophy as a personal trainer
2. Highlight what is special, unique, distinctive, or impressive about you, as a personal trainer
3. Share details of your life, history, and people or events that have shaped you or influenced your decision to become a personal trainer
4. Showcase your certifications and experience with different clients that makes you a stronger candidate than others
5. State the single most compelling reason you can give someone to choose you as their personal trainer

If your website is capable of catching the attention of a potential client, you can assume they will visit your site more than once before they reach out to you to take next steps. If you use online dating as an example, research has shown that:

- People will send at least five online communications before giving out any personal contact information
- People will communicate (online or by phone) for up to three weeks before meeting in person

Regardless of your initial thoughts about building trust on the Internet, establishing a website, that demonstrates your credibility as a personal trainer, is essential to your business. This requires a well thought out marketing strategy, effectively written content and a long term plan for success.

The First 10 Seconds

It's fair to say that the amount of time a visitor spends on a website is a key indicator as to whether or not they will become a personal training client. The more time they spend on the first visit, the more likely they will become a repeat visitor. The more repeat visits they make, the more likely they will contact you and become a personal training client.

Users are always in a hurry when they are on the Internet. Research states that the first ten seconds of page visit is critical for a user's decision to stay or leave. The likelihood of them leaving is very high during these first few seconds because users are extremely skeptical, having encountered poorly designed web pages in the past. Most people assume that most web pages are useless, and they remain skeptical to avoid wasting valuable time in their search for answers.

If the web page survives this first (extremely harsh) ten second judgment, users will look around a little bit longer. However, they're still highly likely to leave during the next 20 seconds of their visit. Only after someone has stayed on a page for 30 seconds or more, the chance of them leaving flatten out. Web page visitors will eventually leave, but at a much slower rate than during the first 30 seconds.

So, roughly speaking, there are two cases here:
1. Bad web pages (which a visitor will leave in less than ten seconds) or,
2. Good web pages (which might get a few minutes of a visitor's

time)

The main difference between the two? Good web pages clearly communicate your value proposition within the first 10 seconds.

A Picture is Worth a Thousand Words

The average adult reads 250 to 300 words per minute. That means you have 41 to 50 words on your web page to get someone's interest and attention. How can you express your value to a web visitor in such a short amount of time?

What you've worked so hard to establish in your business (i.e., your education and training, expensive certifications, the knowledge and experience with clients, volunteer work in your community, etc.) is what makes your brand unique and special. The use of symbols and pictures is incredibly powerful, if used right.

We communicate with symbols every day. Symbols are objects that represent a different meaning without the need for words. Examples include:

Caution   Washroom   Recycling   Wireless   Emergency
                                                Internet (Wi-Fi)   Medical Services

When we see each of these symbols, we recognize them in an instant and they trigger a mental and/or an emotional response.
- We are alerted when we see the caution sign.
- We are informed when we see the washroom, recycling, and wireless internet (Wi-Fi) sign.
- When you have a medical emergency, you feel relieved when you see the Emergency Medical Services (EMS) symbol.

Including the right symbols and imagery can speak volumes to your credibility and expertise from the moment a web visitor lands on your website. For example, a certification from a well known organization speaks to your professionalism and quality before they know anything about you as a person. It is concrete and tangible proof of what you can accomplish as a personal trainer.

Figure 14-1, is an example of a personal training website. It includes useful information and articles for their website visitors and clients. What you will notice is that it doesn't immediately speak to the credibility of the business or the experience they have as fitness professionals that makes them better than their competitors.

If the goal of this website is to educate the visitors on fitness and exercise then they have succeeded. If they want to gain personal training clients,

Figure 14-1: ACTIV Personal Training Home Page (Before)

they will be challenged to get their attention and get them to call back.

Figure 14-2, is an example of an updated website that draws attention to symbols and images that get the web visitor's attention.

1. The feature article highlights one of the Athletic Trainers with the company
2. The video features "Before and After" pictures of clients
3. Certifications highlight the expertise and credibility of the business

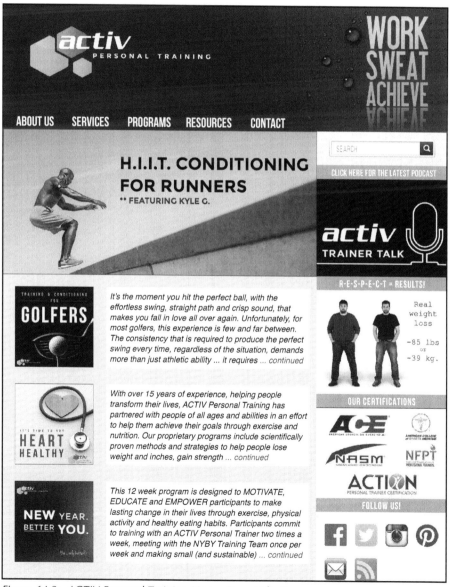

Figure 14-2: ACTIV Personal Training Home Page (After)

In a face-to-face world, knowledge, expertise, experience and credibility are what attracts new clients. On the other hand, the "appearance" of credibility is what motivates website visitors to contact you.

Keep in mind, visitors to your website rely on what they see and read on the Internet to know who you are and what your personal training business is all about. If you don't highlight your strengths in a way that is easily understood by your web visitors, they will never know it and have no reason to contact you. You may be the most amazing personal trainer, with the most comprehensive resume and background, but if you fail to highlight those attributes on your website, nobody will ever know.

Keep it Fresh
Successful websites keep first time web visitors for at least 30 seconds. Really good websites keep them there, perusing through various pages and articles, for two to three minutes. Although that is a good start, the goal is to have unique visitors to your site become repeat visitors.

Using the online dating profile as an example, new content gives visitors a reason to view the profile again. They post new pictures, write new updates, and share information that is new and exciting. They keep the most important information the same (for the first time visitors) but add new content to appeal to the repeat viewers.

Ideas for updating your personal training website (at least once a week) include:

CREATIVE MARKETING IDEA

- Announcing new programs and services being offered (i.e., programs, contests, or challenges)
- Showcase a client who has experienced success
- Write a blog post on relevant fitness, nutrition, and health topics
- Share motivational messages, quotes, or videos

Building trust and credibility on the Internet is possible, but requires a plan and a long term strategy to be successful. Respect the impatient nature of your web visitors, give them a reason to stay on your page for 30 seconds or more, and provide updated content that gives them a reason to keep coming back for more!

Chapter 15:
Understanding Social Media for Your Business

When it comes to business, social media has changed the way companies interact with their potential customers. Business relationships that used to start with a handshake in person, a referral from an existing customer or a handwritten invitation in the mail has now become the "Favorite" on Twitter, the "Share" on Facebook and the "InMail" through LinkedIn.

Social media is beginning to play a significant role in the way businesses operate (big and small) and business owners need to take notice in order to best represent themselves in all ways to potential clients.

What Is Social Media ... Exactly?
Social media is a collection of Internet-based applications that allow people to create, share or exchange information (i.e., ideas, pictures, videos) in online communities and virtual networks. This form of media has been broadly defined to refer to the many inexpensive and widely accessible online tools that enable anyone to publish and access information, collaborate on a common effort.

The main difference between social media and traditional media is in the dialogue between the source and the receiver. Traditional media delivers information from one source (i.e., the television station) to multiple receivers. Social media delivers information from several receivers to several sources, producing an ongoing dialogue that is not limited by physical distance or time.

This is significant because, according to Pew Research Center, social media has increased nearly 1000% over the past decade, as traditional media has seen a massive decline. Social media is a powerful avenue to start a conversation and influence your target audience.

Let's Get <u>REAL</u> About Social Media

Don't kid yourself ... social media is not a fad or a trend. These networks provide a platform for people to exist online. It offers users a legacy beyond their day-to-day lives. Users have an online "heartbeat" that shows they are alive, have a voice and influence on a global scale. This is also true of businesses.

Social media proves to the world that your business is operational, is run by human beings who will actually deliver the personal training services featured on your website, and shows your personality (hopefully one a customer can relate to). These days people are more likely to judge a business by their social media presence instead of their website. This is because social media shows a person's "true colors". A website may showcase the best parts of a company, but social media shows the day-to-day activities of a business and validates whether the information on the website is true (or glaringly false).

Social media marketing can get incredibly confusing because there are so many factors to consider, including:
- Which social sites to choose from
- The best way(s) to engage with users on each social media site
- The various "rules" (and styles) of each platform
- What is the right messaging to get the "right" attention from social media site users
- What is the correct posting frequency to get the greatest response
- How to get the attention of the billions of people hanging out on social media so they are interested in what you have to sell

The fact that you have one or more social media accounts (and post on a regular basis) doesn't guarantee your social media marketing will be a success. People are quick to believe that having lots of fans, likes or followers is a reflection of their social media success. Unfortunately, those numbers mean you "may" have an audience but if you're not generating conversations, adding new subscribers to your website, or making any additional money, then what you're doing (or not doing) has failed.

Creating a Powerful Social Media Strategy

Establishing a social media strategy is more than just posting an update informing people that a new program or workshop is available. It's more than just sharing relevant information. A social media strategy is successful when you are able to engage and interact with your target audience on a consistent basis.

Sounds simple, right?

The honest truth is the majority of social media strategies fail. They fail for the exact same reasons any other traditional marketing strategy would fall short:

- The values are mismatched
- No consistency
- No variety
- Talking (but not listening)
- Lack of monitoring or evaluating

Values Mismatched

Assuming you read the first book in the series, "The Business of Personal Training: Essential Guide for the Successful Personal Trainer", you would have already established the core values, mission statement, goals and brand image of your business. With all of these essential parts of your business in place you would assume your social media strategy would be easy to execute.

Unfortunately, many business owners forget to refer back to the core values of their business when they use social media. For example:

- If one of your core values is sustainability and "going green" but you post a video on Facebook that is sponsored by a bottled water company, that would contradict your values.

- If one of your core values is providing custom designed programs and personalized care for every client but you promote the release of a generic workout video on Instagram it would also contradict your values.

Your core values should be at the heart of everything you communicate via social media. It is your barometer and gauge that guides the content and social media objectives.

No Consistency
Any social media campaign requires consistency. You want to take someone on a journey and you need to leave crumbs behind for them to follow. For the most part people like to "snack" on social media versus sit down to Thanksgiving dinner. They just want a "taste" of something and then move on to something else. Your goal is to provide valuable content in bite sized morsels to fulfil the audience's needs and keep them coming back for more.

As for how frequent you should share content ... that is a tougher question to answer, requires research into your target demographic and is dependent on which social media outlet you use. A few tools that provide valuable information include:
- Google Alerts (www.google.com/alerts)
- Hootsuite (www.hootsuite.com)
- TweetDeck (www.tweetdeck.com)
- Social Mention (www.socialmention.com)

Figure 15-1 outlines the ideal posting days (and times) for specific social media networks that have been validated by research and trending analysis.

No Variety
Although creating content on a regular basis (sometimes multiple times a day) is difficult, it is even more challenging to develop unique and interesting media. With so many people competing for attention via social media why would they like, share or favorite your content if it's the same as everybody else's?

When coming up with ideas try and create ones that are unique and different. At the very least, your concepts should be tailored to your specific target audience. For example, if a celebrity image has gone viral on social media, use the same image but change the caption to match your business needs, core values or personal (yet professional) sense of humor.

Talking (But Not Listening)

The whole purpose of social media (and what users expect) is to promote conversations and personal engagement. People don't want to be sold on social media and will quickly tune you out and never come back because of it.

Instead of talking "at" your audience, engage them by asking questions and encouraging feedback. Give the audience a chance to share their thoughts and ideas (i.e., what they liked or disliked) or suggestions for the future.

Lack of Monitoring or Evaluating

In the end, what it all boils down to is ... lack of monitoring or evaluating the social media campaign. Even if you've done your homework and identified your target audience and the right network to deliver your message, you still need to keep an eye on how effective your content is and how it's being received.

For example, you've identified Facebook the best network to grow your personal training business. In order to ensure this is the case you need to ask yourself the following questions:
- How many likes or shares does your content receive?
- Are people commenting on the posts?
- Are you making any money because of your Facebook content?
- Are you getting any new subscribers to your website because of your Facebook posts?

If the content that you're promoting isn't producing quantifiable results, you need reevaluate your strategy ... otherwise you are just wasting your time and money.

The Bottom Line

Social media is here to stay. There is no indication that it is going anywhere or that it's value is going to diminish when it comes to business. Although social media sites are essentially "FREE" it doesn't mean they are worthless. In fact, they will most certainly yield more power and influence as time goes on.

Social media should not be taken lightly, and takes a significant amount of time to learn and master. Be patient. Do the work. Be true to your business and represent your brand with integrity. Taking the time to do this right will reward you beyond belief.

	FACEBOOK	TWITTER	INSTAGRAM
HOW OFTEN	**2** posts per day	**3** posts per day	**1.5** posts per day
POPULAR DAYS	Wednesday Thursday Friday Saturday Sunday	Monday Tuesday Wednesday Thursday Friday	Monday Tuesday Wednesday Thursday
BEST TIME(S)	1pm to 4pm *(on weekdays)* 12pm to 1pm *(on weekends)*	12pm to 3pm	Any time
WORST TIME(S)	Weekends before 8am and after 8pm	Everyday after 8pm and Fridays after 3pm	Everyday between 3pm and 4pm
TIPS	Because people are happier on Fridays, post upbeat or funny content.	Business-to-Business (B2B) engagement is better during the workweek. Business-to-Consumer (B2C) engagement is better on the weekends.	Posting video will get 34% more interactions (any day between 9pm and 8am).

Source:
- *The Ultimate Best Times to Post on Social Media (2015), www.coschedule.com*
- *The Best Times to Post on Facebook, Twitter, LinkedIn and Other Social Media Sites (2016), www.hubspot.com*

Figure 15-1: Posting to Social Media - Recommendations

Chapter 16:
Setting Up Your Social Media Accounts

Now that you understand the power of social media, it's time to set up your social media accounts! Not all social media platforms are right for your business, but the following are important social media sites (with high volumes of traffic) that you should consider as you build out your business website:

- Facebook
- Google+
- Instagram
- LinkedIn
- Twitter

FACEBOOK (www.facebook.com)

Facebook is a social networking website that allows users to connect and share information with people in their network (i.e., family and friends). This online platform provides robust tools that allow users to connect and share a wide variety of information with the people they care about ... in real time.

Unlike a private text message or email to an individual, Facebook allows users to send messages and post status updates publicly, for all connected friends and family members to see. In addition, these messages and status updates are also seen by the network of each friend and family member. In the end this platform is intended to be very social and extremely public.

Because Facebook has over one billion monthly active users, businesses are finding ways to leverage this online community. Businesses use Facebook pages to share their stories and connect with people in new ways. Like a Facebook profile you can customize pages by publishing stories, hosting events, sharing images and videos, and more. People who "Like" your page (including their friends) can see the updates on your page in their News Feed.

To set up your Facebook business page, follow these steps:
1. Go to www.facebook.com.
2. Log into your personal Facebook account and select "Create a Page" (located on the left side navigate under "Pages"). A personal Facebook account is not necessary. You can set up a Facebook business page from the Facebook Sign Up page.
3. Complete your Facebook business profile (i.e., category, business name address, phone number, description, website, links, etc.).
4. Customize your Facebook Page (i.e., profile picture and cover photo).
5. Choose a "short name" to customize your Facebook URL (i.e., http://www.facebook.com/yourwebsite).
6. Populate your page with a variety of content:
   - Status updates
   - Photo with description
   - Link with description
   - Video with description
   - Event page
   - Location check-in

GOOGLE+ (www.plus.google.com)
Google + is the second largest social network, with over 500 million users (but access to over 2.5 billion accounts). Essentially anyone who has a Gmail account has a Google+ profile (but only 20 percent of them are actively using it).

Google+ is not meant to compete against Facebook or Twitter. It is designed to evolve the way people connect and relate with one another using the power of the Internet. Much like how Gmail changed the way people communicate and share information (i.e., Google Calendar, Google Docs, etc.), Google+ is designed to remove borders and language barriers to connect like-minded people online.

Google+ is important for your business website for the following reasons:
- It is promoted by the biggest technology company in the world (Google), and it doesn't do anything that doesn't go BIG!
- Everything that you post on Google+ is indexed by Google (which has an effect on search engine results)
- You get access to everything Google has to offer (i.e., Google, Gmail, Youtube, Google Maps, etc.)
- Your Google experience is tailored to how you specify your needs and what your interests are (which means it does the same for all Google+ users)
- The "+1" button gives people the opportunity to establish what's trendy (with REAL votes)
- You can add authorship to your content which builds trust among users (which increases clicks, traffic and search volume of your site)
- Google Hangouts offers an opportunity to connect with your potential customers and/or audience free of charge (i.e., online conferences, debates and live demonstrations)

To set up your Google+ account, follow these steps:
1. Go to www.plus.google.com.
2. If you have a Google account you can sign in (if not, click on "Create an Account").
3. When you have set up an account with Google, continue to sign in with Google+.
4. When you first log into Google+ you will need to setup your profile. Click on "Create Profile".
5. Complete your personal information and a username that everyone will see (it recommended that you use a name that relates to your authority website or brand).
6. Add a photo to your profile (you may want to use your logo).
7. Add other websites and links to pages you've contributed writing

to in the "Links" section of your profile.

8. Connect with other Google+ users (your customers, business partners, competitors or peers, people you know, etc.).
9. Share content on your profile page.
10. Join a Google Hangout and establish yourself in circles of influence.

Be sure to explore all the functionality and resources available as a Google+ user. There are many tools that can help you expand your reach through Google.

INSTAGRAM (www.instagram.com)

Instagram is a free online photo sharing social network platform that allows members to upload, edit and share photos with:

- Other Instagram users (including "followers")
- Your Twitter followers
- Your Facebook friends
- Your Tumblr, Foursquare and Flickr profiles

Instagram allows users for find compelling content and other user accounts with hashtags (a word preceded by a "#", used to categorize information into topics on social networks).

At this time, Instagram is proving to be incredibly important for any kind of business because it is where regular people find (and judge) the visual identity of a business. Without a strong Instagram presence, companies risk being ignored or forgotten, especially among the next generation of customers.

To set up your Instagram account, follow these steps:

1. Download the Instagram mobile app to your mobile device (i.e., smartphone or tablet).
2. Choose a username that represents your brand.
3. Complete a short and concise bio (limited to 150 characters), that should also include any branded hashtags.
4. Include your website URL.
5. Include a profile photo (i.e., the website or business logo).
6. Start following people (find customers, business partners,

competitors or peers, people you know, etc.).

7. Post images to your profile (keep them consistent to your authority website brand), be creative and include relevant branded hashtags in your captions.

TWITTER (www.twitter.com)

Twitter is a short message communication tool where users send out messages (aka., "tweets"), up to 140 characters in length, to people who subscribe to your account (aka., "followers"). Tweets can include text, a link to any web content (i.e., blog post, page on a website, document, etc.), image/ photograph or video.

To set up your Twitter account (used to market your authority website), follow these steps:

1. Go to www.twitter.com.
2. Choose a username that represents your brand.
3. Add a profile image and cover photo.
4. Complete your Twitter Profile (include location, authority website and bio).
5. Start following people (find customers, business partners, competitors or peers, people you know, etc.).
6. Start communicating.
   - Tweet: a message you send out to everyone who follows you
   - @Reply: a message you send out as a reply to a message you received via a "mention"
   - Mention: a message you send out that mentions another Twitter username
   - Direct Message: a message you send privately to another Twitter user (can only be sent to someone who follows you)
   - Retweet: a message created and sent out by someone else that you then share with the people who follow you
7. Install the Twitter mobile app on your mobile device (i.e., smartphone, tablet).

Now that you have your social media accounts set up, it's time to put them to good use!

PART FOUR:
SAMPLE MARKETING CAMPAIGNS

Congratulations! You've survived the first three sections of the book ... and are ready to take the next step! The concepts and information is challenging and can take time to digest but you now know:

- What marketing is.
- How it (when done properly) can significantly grow your personal training business.
- The importance of having a brand message that is unique, genuine and relatable to your target market.
- Marketing takes time, effort and adequate planning to be successful.

Now, it's time to take this knowledge and understanding and ... put it into ACTION!

Your comprehension of marketing has already put you ahead of the vast majority of trainers who will sabotage the true potential of their business. These trainers dedicate the majority of their valuable time working **IN** the business (i.e., training clients, teaching classes and providing services) and very little time **ON** the business (i.e., planning for success, evaluating performance and taking the necessary steps to grow).

In fact, these personal trainers display the same personality traits as a typical personal training client ... people who are not happy with their current state (i.e., how they look and feel), know they need to do "something" (i.e., exercise, eat better, make healthier lifestyle choices) to improve but are not educated or motivated to actually do the work! They choose not to take the steps forward (on their own) because they aren't confident in this area and don't like feeling "uncomfortable".

Sound familiar?

For even the most experienced marketers, creating an effective marketing plan for any business takes a significant amount of time and a concentrated effort. This is not something that is done overnight or on a whim. It requires planning and preparation to successfully implement each month's marketing program and strategy.

The following section provides samples of different marketing campaigns a personal training business could implement to grow the business. Each marketing campaign includes a comprehensive outline, grassroots activities, digital media strategies and social media tactics.

SAMPLE #1

January, the first month of the year, symbolizes a new start, new beginnings, and New Year's resolutions! This marketing strategy is designed to promote personal training services and appeal to a different demographic of clientele (individuals who are athletes or weekend warriors that are seeking the knowledge and expertise of specialized strength and conditioning coaches) who are motivated to take the necessary action to improve their health and fitness early in the new year.

Target Audience
The target audience includes people living within 20 miles of the ACTIV Personal Training location, who are over the age of 14 years, are not happy with their current physique (body shape), are seeking expert advice from personal trainers focused on results and are looking for effective solutions to help them achieve their goals in a specific timeline.

Marketing Message
Another year has gone by and you still don't like the body you see in the mirror? Let ACTIV Personal Training help you reveal a "NEW YOU" in 2016!

With over 15 years of experience, helping people transform their lives, ACTIV Personal Training has partnered with people of all ages and abilities in an effort to help them achieve their goals through exercise and nutrition. Our proprietary programs include scientifically proven methods and strategies to help people lose weight and inches, gain strength and improve performance, and recover from injuries with great results.

Duration of the Program
- 12 weeks (January to March/April)

Services Provided

- Comprehensive fitness assessments (pre and post)
- Complete nutritional assessment
- Customized meal plan (12 weeks)
- 24 personal training sessions (60 minutes each; 2 times per week)
- NYBY Training Team meetings (60 minutes; once per week)
- "NEW YEAR. BETTER YOU." Guide (workbook by ACTIV Personal Training)
- Fit Food: Eating Well for Life (book by Ellen Haas; Kindle edition)

<u>Note</u>: *This requires the production/purchase of the books listed above.*

List of Promotional Materials

1. One page flyer (8.5" x 11")
2. Email template (current clients and opt-in database)
3. Landing page or blog post (www.activ-pt.com)
4. Social media communications (Facebook, Twitter and Instagram)
5. ACTIV Personal Training t-shirt and gear (prizes)

One Page Flyer

The one-page flyer (8.5" x 11") should include the following:

1. Company logo
2. Contact information (address, phone number, website, and email address)
3. Program name, details and key selling features
4. Deadline for sign up and/or start date for the program
5. Cost of the complete program and/or the total cost savings of purchasing the program versus individual services
6. Call to action (i.e., "Limited Spots Available")

Landing Page or Blog Post

The website should include a promotional landing page and/or blog post providing information about the ACTIV Personal Training program and should include the following:

1. Program name, details and key selling features
2. Link to testimonial of client who participated in the program last

year
3. Link to download One Page Flyer (8.5" x 11")
4. Link to "Fit Food: Eating Well for Life" (Kindle edition)
5. Link to Shopping Cart to purchase program
6. Image of ACTIV Personal Training t-shirt and gear (optional)
7. Call to action (i.e., "Click HERE to secure your spot today!")

Grassroots Marketing Strategies

1. Key Influencer(s)

   Identify one (1) key influencer in your community who has either shown interest in the program or would greatly benefit from the program. Offer them the complete 12 week program at no cost for their participation in your marketing efforts. This individual is then responsible for completing the program, before and after fitness assessments (including photos), and a written and/or video testimonial of their experience on the program. A media release and consent form is recommended.

   It is important that this candidate be chosen very carefully as your investment (in time and effort) is only as good as the results this participant achieves at the end of the program and the information (i.e., results, images, and testimonial) you can include in your marketing efforts.

2. Promotional Products (Giveaways)

   As a part of the 12 week program, all participants receive an ACTIV Personal Training t-shirt at the completion of the program. T-shirts are also given away as a part of the Facebook and Twitter social media campaigns.

Note: This promotion requires the design and purchase of t-shirts for distribution.

IS YOUR "HAPPY NEW YEAR" NOT AS HAPPY AS YOU WOULD LIKE?

ARE YOU WANTING TO LOOK AND FEEL BETTER?

ARE YOU AFRAID TO START ANOTHER PROGRAM ... ONLY TO BE DISAPPOINTED AGAIN?

ARE YOU LOOKING FOR HELP ... BUT DON'T KNOW WHERE TO GO OR WHO TO TRUST?

Join the "NEW YEAR. BETTER YOU." (NYBY) Training Team for a 12 week journey that will start your year off right!

This 12 week program is designed to **MOTIVATE, EDUCATE** and **EMPOWER** participants to make lasting change in their lives through exercise, physical activity and healthy eating habits. Participants commit to training with an ACTIV Personal Trainer two times a week, meeting with the NYBY Training Team once per week and making small (and sustainable) changes to their lifestyle and eating habits.

WHAT'S INCLUDED:
- Comprehensive fitness assessments (pre and post)
- Complete nutritional assessment
- Customized meal plan (12 weeks)
- 24 personal training sessions (60 minutes each; 2 times per week)
- NYBY Training Team meetings (60 minutes; once per week)
- "NEW YEAR. BETTER YOU." Guide (workbook by ACTIV Personal Training)
- Fit Food: Eating Well for Life (book by Ellen Haas; Kindle edition)

CONDITIONS:
- Maximum of 12 participants included in the NYBY training program (January 25 to April 10)
- NYBY Training Team will meet every Thursday from 7:30 to 8:30pm (at ACTIV Personal Training)
- Each participant will have set days and times for their weekly personal training sessions (changes require a minimum of 72 hours notice and subject to availability)

DEADLINE:
- Sunday, January 24th (or when 12 spots are filled)

INVESTMENT
- The all-inclusive NYBY results-based training program is $2,000.00 (a retail value of $2,500.00).

SPOTS ARE LIMITED! SIGN UP TODAY!

FOR MORE INFORMATION VISIT

www.activ-pt.com

ACTIV Personal Training
123 Anywhere Street
Smallville, CA 12345
P: (123) 456-7890

Figure S1-1: "New Year. Better You." Handout

Be sure to print at least 500 sheets (8.5″ x 11″) to hand out during your campaign:
- To current clients
- For clients to share with friends/family members
- At speaking events or workshops
- At partner locations (businesses that you promote and vice versa)

ABOUT US   SERVICES   PROGRAMS   RESOURCES   CONTACT

NEW YEAR. BETTER YOU. (2016)

December 10, 2016 By: Andrea Oh - 4 Comments

LIKE IT? SHARE IT!

- IS YOUR "HAPPY NEW YEAR" NOT AS HAPPY AS YOU WOULD LIKE?
- ARE YOU WANTING TO LOOK AND FEEL BETTER?
- ARE YOU AFRAID TO START ANOTHER PROGRAM ... ONLY TO BE DISAPPOINTED AGAIN?

Join the "NEW YEAR. BETTER YOU." (NYBY) Training Team for a 12 week journey that will start your year off right!

This 12 week program is designed to MOTIVATE, EDUCATE and EMPOWER participants to make lasting change in their lives through exercise, physical activity and healthy eating habits. Participants commit to training with an ACTIV Personal Trainer two times a week, meeting with the NYBY Training Team once per week and making small (and sustainable) changes to their lifestyle and eating habits.

WHAT'S INCLUDED:
- Comprehensive fitness assessments (pre and post)
- Complete nutritional assessment and customized meal plan (12 weeks)
- 24 personal training sessions (60 minutes each; 2 times per week)
- NYBY Training Team meetings (60 minutes; once per week)
- "NEW YEAR. BETTER YOU." Guide (workbook by ACTIV Personal Training)
- Fit Food: Eating Well for Life (book by Ellen Haas; Kindle edition)

CONDITIONS:
- Maximum of 12 participants included in the NYBY training program (January 25 to April 10)
- NYBY Training Team will meet every Thursday from 7:30 to 8:30pm (at ACTIV Personal Training)
- Each participant will have set days and times for their weekly personal training sessions (changes require a minimum of 72 hours notice and subject to availability)

DEADLINE:
Sunday, January 24th (or when 12 spots are filled)

CLICK HERE TO DOWNLOAD THE BROCHURE OR EMAIL US TODAY!

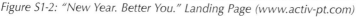

Figure S1-2: "New Year. Better You." Landing Page (www.activ-pt.com)

Be sure to post the URL to this page on all of your social media networks (at least once a week):
- Facebook (personal page)
- Facebook (business page)
- Twitter
- Instagram (unique image to promote this page)
- Google+

| Send | Reply | Quote | Responses | Attach | Signatures | Save | | Sidebar |

Andrea Oh <trainer@activ-pt.com> ⌄

To:

Cc:

Bcc:

Reply-To:

Subject: Happy Holidays!

| Variable Width ⌄ | A↓ A↑ | ■ a | B I U | | ⟨⟩ 𝕀ₓ |

Happy Holidays, <NAME>!

I hope you are getting a chance to spend time with family and friends this holiday season (which obviously included lots of good food and festivities)!

Now that we are coming ot the end of the year and January is just around the corner (the beginning of a new year and ... New Year's resolutions), my schedule is already starting to fill up with many of my regular clients eager to get back into regular training sessions. In addition, I have already gotten a handful of new clients wanting to get started!

As a courtesy to you, I wanted to reach out and make sure that if you were looking to schedule some sessions in the next 12 weeks, that you let me know as soon as possible. The reason for booking in advance is because the "New Year. Better You." (NYBY) program is BACK!!

In case you are not familiar, we have run the NYBY program the last three years with several of my clients seeing incredible results in just 12 weeks! It runs from January 25th to April 10th this year. I take 12 participants to join the NYBY Training Team. The team members commit to personal training with me twice a week and meeting once a week as a group for an educational workshop and support session. This program also includes fitness assessments (before and after), a nutrition assessment and 12 week customized meal plan, workbooks and more! What's even better is that participants get $500 in bonus products and services if they commit to the program!

As you can imagine, this program is very popular and it will take up a portion of my schedule up until April.

If you would like to schedule your appointments, please give me a call at (123) 456-7890 or email me at trainer@activ-pt.com. In addition, if you are interested in being a part of the NYBY Training Team DEFINITELY let me know! It would be great to have you join us!

Regardless, thank you for your ongoing support and commitment to your health and fitness.

Have a wonderful holidays and I look forward to speaking with you soon!

Andrea.
--
ANDREA OH
Owner & Head Strength and Conditioning Coach

Figure S1-3: "New Year. Better You." Email to Clients

As a follow up to this email, assuming clients that are not currently training with you will receive this, give each recipient on this list a phone call. You can easily reference this email as the basis of your call, cultivate a meaningful conversation, and help identify whether (or not) this program is ideal for this particular client.

FITNESS TIP OF THE DAY
Exercise is not something that most people naturally include in their daily lives. Regardless of how good it is for you, most people need to set goals to motivate them to stay active and do what's necessary to stay healthy and stay fit.

A goal, especially when it comes to exercise and physical activity, is USELESS without a reason for doing it. A goal is like a destination on a road map. You are in one city and your goal is to get to another one that is over a thousand miles away. The question is not what route to take, or your mode of transportation (ie. plane, train, car, bike). It's knowing how to fuel the engine to get you from point A to point B. Without fuel (food or gasoline) ... you aren't going anywhere!

When it comes to setting any goal (and successfully achieving it), most people ask themselves, "How am I going to do this?" Unfortunately, they don't ask the most important question ... "Why am I doing this?"

Many people identify a goal and create a program to follow to help them get there but they don't take the time to understand what will motivate them to make it through the long journey. They don't peel back the layers to uncover what is truly motivating them to make a change. For example, someone may have a goal to:
>> Lose weight because they want to look and feel better.
>> Fit into the clothes that are too small because they don't have the money to buy new clothes.
>> Eat a healthier diet because their doctor told them they are at high risk for coronary heart disease and type II diabetes.
>> Quit smoking because they want to be able to play with their children without huffing and puffing.

Take the time to identify the reasons why you want to incorporate exercise and physical activity into your daily life. Knowing why you want to change will help you to be more accountable to your actions and make you more aware of the negative consequences if you don't stick to the program.

By digging deeper and understanding your true motivations for your actions, you will be more successful in adhering to your fitness program and achieving your long term goals!

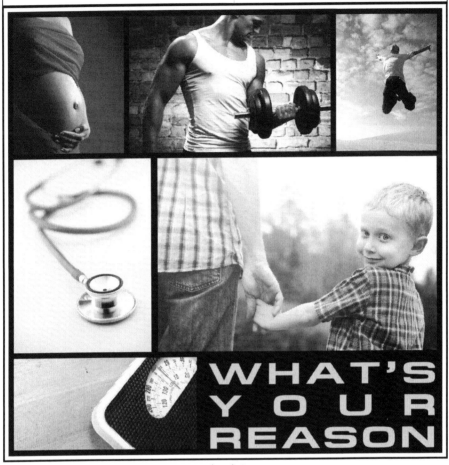

Figure S1-4: "New Year. Better You." Facebook Post

CREATIVE MARKETING IDEA

Although Facebook is useful, it doesn't guarantee that everyone who likes your page will see every post. If you happen to have clients as "friends" on Facebook, you can "share" this post in a private message. This will provide a higher percentage of readers for any post on your page.

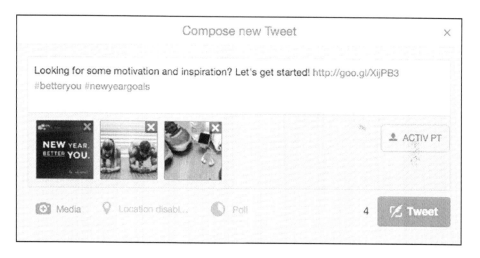

Figure S1-5: "New Year. Better You." Tweets

NEW YEAR.
BETTER YOU.

(You ... only better!)

activpersonaltraining Our famous 12 week transformation program is BACK! "NEW YEAR. BETTER YOU." is ready to change lives starting on January 24th. Check out the link on our profile page (or http://goo.gl/V9Yuig) for more information! #newyearbetteryou #transformation2016 #12weeks #smallville

 Add a comment...   ◌ ◌ ◌

Figure S1-6: "New Year. Better You." Instagram Post

132

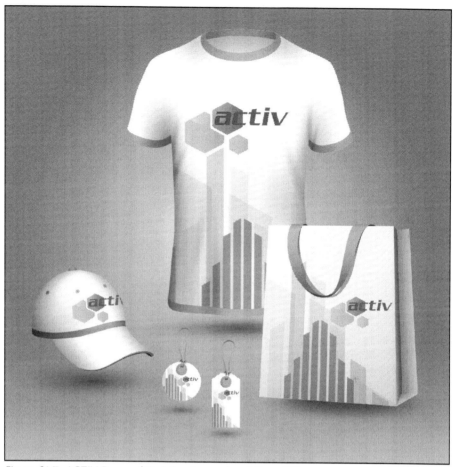

Figure S1-7: ACTIV Personal Training Promotional Gear (S1)

You, your staff (if you have other trainers working for you) and your clients are your best marketing and advertising. Wear your logo with pride and reward others for their hard work and dedication with unique gear!

Be sure to choose apparel and accessories that match the quality and integrity of your business. If you are providing services at a higher price point than your competitors, ensure the same quality is consistent in anything tangible that represents your business (i.e., business cards, handouts, t-shirts, hats, etc.). If you charge a high price for training but use sub-par materials, the inconsistency is evident to your audience.

Marketing Checklist

1. Produce one page handouts and/or signage. ☐
2. Produce landing page (or blog post) on website. ☐
3. Get marketing and promotional materials printed. ☐
4. Send out email to current client database. ☐
5. Start grassroots marketing initiatives. ☐
6. Produce a minimum of five (5) Facebook posts to promote during the advertising period. ☐
7. Produce a minimum of ten (10) Tweets to promote during the advertising period. ☐
8. Send reminder email to current client database one week prior to program start date. ☐
9. Evaluate the marketing strategy. ☐

SAMPLE #2

IT'S TIME TO GET
HEART HEALTHY

The first three months of the year are "peak times" for personal trainers. Although some people are ready to start their "New Year's resolution" program in January, some need a little bit more time (and convincing) to get started. In addition, February is also the month dedicated to the heart (i.e., Valentine's Day and American Heart Month).

To capitalize on the messages already present in the media, this marketing strategy is designed to educate people about the benefits exercise, proper nutrition and the prevention of heart disease. The goal is to create awareness by providing valuable education, useful information and products and services that offer a solution to the problems outlined.

Target Audience
The target audience includes people living within 20 miles of the ACTIV Personal Training location, who are over the age of 14 years and are interested in achieving long term health (specifically preventing heart disease and stroke).

Marketing Message
Did you know ...
- In the US, 155 million adults (68%) and 37 million children (49%) are considered overweight and obese
- An estimated 20 million adults have diabetes, an addition 8 million have undiagnosed diabetes, and about 87 million have prediabetes
- According to the American Heart Association, regular physical activity can lower your blood pressure and improve your cholesterol levels and active people with high blood pressure, high blood cholesterol, and chronic diseases like heart disease are less likely to die prematurely than inactive people with these conditions.

Interested in learning more? Join ACTIV Personal Training for one of our informative "Heart Healthy" workshops during the month of February!

With over 15 years of experience, helping people transform their lives, ACTIV Personal Training has been there to coach people of all ages and abilities, helping them achieve their goals through focused exercise and nutrition. Our proprietary programs include scientifically proven methods and strategies to help people lose weight and inches, gain strength, improve performance and recover from injuries with exceptional results.

Duration of the Strategy
- 4 weeks (February 1 to 28/29)

Services Provided
- 2 x "Heart Healthy" complimentary workshops (February 14th at 12:00pm and 6:30pm)
- WORKING 9 TO 5: Heart Healthy Lunch Solutions (Kindle edition)
- DISCOUNT CODE: Personal Training Sessions for $50.00 (regularly $75.00; limit of 5 sessions)

Promotional Material(s)
1. One page flyer (8.5" x 11")
2. Email template (current clients and opt-in database)
3. Landing page or blog post (www.activ-pt.com)
4. Social media communications (Facebook, Twitter and Instagram)
5. ACTIV Personal Training t-shirt and gear (giveaways)

One Page Flyer
The one-page flyer (8.5" x 11") should include the following:
1. Company logo
2. Contact information (address, phone number, website, and email address)
3. Workshop name, details and benefits to attendees
4. Deadline for sign up (i.e., RSVP to trainer@activ-pt.com)
5. Call to action (i.e., "Limited Spots Available")

Landing Page or Blog Post

The website should include a promotional landing page and/or blog post providing information about the complimentary "Heart Healthy" workshops and should include the following:

1. Workshop name, details and benefits to attendees
2. Links to supporting evidence and references
3. Link to download One Page Flyer (8.5" x 11")
4. Link to "WORKING 9 TO 5: Heart Healthy Lunch Solutions" information page
5. Link to Shopping Cart to purchase personal training sessions (using Discount Code)
6. Image of ACTIV Personal Training t-shirt and gear (optional)
7. Call to action (i.e., "Click HERE to secure your spot today!")

Grassroots Marketing Strategies

1. Key Influencer(s)

   Identify at least five (5) businesses in your local area who have clients who would benefit from the "Heart Healthy" workshop. Examples include:

   - Local medical professionals (i.e., doctors, chiropractors, nutritionists)
   - Grocery store (specializing in produce and organic foods)
   - Restaurants with "Heart Healthy" menus
   - Sporting goods/specialty fitness stores
   - Local branch of the American Heart Association

   Reach out and invite them to attend and/or participate in the event. Find out if they would be willing to promote the workshop at their place of business. If they find value in your event they may be willing to contribute healthy snacks, giveaways, or coupons redeemed at a later date (to bring them back at another time). This creates more value for your attendees and makes it more memorable for your participants (at no additional cost to you).

2. Workshop Locations

   Of the businesses you have approached to participate in the workshop, choose one to be the event location. Choose wisely as the location must be one that is convenient and appealing to the

IT'S TIME TO GET
HEART HEALTHY

DID YOU KNOW ...
- In the US, 155 million adults (68%) and 37 million children (49%) are overweight and obese
- An estimated 20 million adults have diabetes, an addition 8 million have undiagnosed diabetes, and about 87 million have prediabetes
- According to the American Heart Association, regular physical activity can lower your blood pressure and improve your cholesterol levels and active people with high blood pressure, high blood cholesterol, and chronic diseases like heart disease are less likely to die prematurely than inactive people with these conditions.

Interested in learning more? Join ACTIV Personal Training for one of our informative "Heart Healthy" workshops on February 14th (12:00pm and 6:30pm)!

With over 15 years of experience, helping people transform their lives, ACTIV Personal Training has partnered with people of all ages and abilities in an effort to help them achieve their goals through exercise and nutrition. Our proprietary programs include scientifically proven methods and strategies to help people lose weight and inches, gain strength and improve performance, and recover from injuries with great results.

DATE:
- Saturday, February 14th (Valentine's Day)

TIME(S):
- 12:00pm to 1:30pm @ ACTIV Personal Training
- 6:30pm to 8:00pm @ FIT KITCHEN (33 High Street SE; in McKenzie Towne Village)

RSVP BY:
- Friday, February 13th @ 8:00pm

PARTICIPANTS WILL RECEIVE A HEART HEALTHY RECIPE BOOK,
EXCLUSIVE DISCOUNTS ON ACTIV PERSONAL TRAINING SERVICES, AND
A CHANCE TO WIN A $500 FIT KITCHEN PRIZE PACK!

FOR MORE INFORMATION VISIT

www.activ-pt.com

ACTIV Personal Training
123 Anywhere Street
Smallville, CA 12345
P: (123) 456-7890

Figure S2-1: "Heart Healthy Workshop" Handout

Be sure to print at least 500 sheets (8.5" x 11") to hand out during your campaign:
- To current clients
- For clients to share with friends/family members
- At speaking events or workshops
- At partner locations (businesses that you promote and vice versa)

ABOUT US   SERVICES   PROGRAMS   RESOURCES   CONTACT

HEART HEALTHY WORKSHOP

January 31, 2016   By: Andrea Oh - 3 Comments

LIKE IT? SHARE IT!

DID YOU KNOW ...
- In the US, 155 million adults (68%) and 37 million children (49%) are overweight and obese
- An estimated 20 million adults have diabetes, an addition 8 million have undiagnosed diabetes, and about 87 million have prediabetes
- According to the American Heart Association, regular physical activity can lower your blood pressure and improve your cholesterol levels and active people with high blood pressure, high blood cholesterol, and chronic diseases like heart disease are less likely to die prematurely than inactive people with these conditions.

Interested in learning more? Join ACTIV Personal Training for one of our informative "Heart Healthy" workshops on February 14th (12:00pm and 6:30pm)!

With over 15 years of experience, helping people transform their lives, ACTIV Personal Training has partnered with people of all ages and abilities in an effort to help them achieve their goals through exercise and nutrition. Our proprietary programs include scientifically proven methods and strategies to help people lose weight and inches, gain strength and improve performance, and recover from injuries with great results.

DATE:
- Saturday, February 14th (Valentine's Day)

TIME(S):
- 12:00pm to 1:30pm @ ACTIV Personal Training
- 6:30pm to 8:00pm @ FIT KITCHEN (33 High Street SE; in McKenzie Towne Village)

RSVP BY:
- Friday, February 13th @ 8:00pm

CLICK HERE TO DOWNLOAD THE BROCHURE OR EMAIL US TODAY!

Figure S2-2: "Heart Healthy Workshop" Landing Page (www.activ-pt.com)

Be sure to post the URL to this page on all of your social media networks (at least once a week):
- Facebook (personal page)
- Facebook (business page)
- Twitter
- Instagram (unique image to promote this page)
- Google+

| Send | Reply | Quote | Responses | Attach | Signatures | Save | | Sidebar |

Andrea Oh <trainer@activ-pt.com> ∨

To:

Cc:

Bcc:

Reply-To:

Subject: It's Time to Get "Heart Healthy"!

| Variable Width ∨ | A↓ A↑ | ■ | a | B | I | U | | ∞ | </> | Iₓ |

<NAME>,

February is more than just for Valentine's Day ... it's also a month dedicated to taking care of your heart!

DID YOU KNOW ...
- In the US, 155 million adults (68%) and 37 million children (49%) are overweight and obese
- An estimated 20 million adults have diabetes, an addition 8 million have undiagnosed diabetes, and about 87 million have prediabetes
- According to the American Heart Association, regular physical activity can lower your blood pressure and improve your cholesterol levels and active people with high blood pressure, high blood cholesterol, and chronic diseases like heart disease are less likely to die prematurely than inactive people with these conditions.

Interested in learning more? Join ACTIV Personal Training for one of our informative "Heart Healthy" workshops on February 14th (12:00pm and 6:30pm)!

With over 15 years of experience, helping people transform their lives, ACTIV Personal Training has partnered with people of all ages and abilities in an effort to help them achieve their goals through exercise and nutrition. Our proprietary programs include scientifically proven methods and strategies to help people lose weight and inches, gain strength and improve performance, and recover from injuries with great results.

DATE:
Saturday, February 14th (Valentine's Day)

TIME(S):
12:00pm to 1:30pm @ ACTIV Personal Training
6:30pm to 8:00pm @ FIT KITCHEN (33 High Street SE; in McKenzie Towne Village)

RSVP BY:
Friday, February 13th @ 8:00pm

If you would like to RSVP for this event, please give me a call at (123) 456-7890 or email me at trainer@activ-pt.com

Regardless, thank you for your ongoing support and commitment to your health and fitness.

Have a wonderful holidays and I look forward to speaking with you soon!

Andrea.

ANDREA OH
Owner & Head Strength and Conditioning Coach

activ
PERSONAL TRAINING
www.activ-pt.com

Figure S2-3: "Heart Healthy Workshop" Email to Clients

As a follow up to this email, assuming clients that are not currently training with you will receive this, give each recipient on this list a phone call. You can easily reference this email as the basis of your call, cultivate a meaningful conversation, and help identify whether (or not) this program is ideal for this particular client.

FITNESS TIP OF THE DAY:
Don't ignore the importance of food and nutrition when it comes to achieving your health and fitness goals.

Most people focus the majority of their efforts on exercise when it comes to a fitness goal (i.e. losing weight, losing inches, getting stronger). This is one of the reasons why some people workout diligently and wonder why they aren't seeing the physical results they are hoping to achieve. What most people forget is the fact that food and nutrition plays a large part in getting results. It actually plays a more significant role than exercise alone!

Food for thought ... we make eating our "primary activity" an average of three times a day (not including the times we snack while doing other things at the same time). Depending on your schedule you may only make time to exercise three times in a week. You have more opportunities to make "better" decisions that benefit your health and fitness goals every time you eat versus the times you choose to be physically active. That means that in an average week you will:
>> Eat 28 to 35 meals and/or snacks
>> Drink 14 to 28 additional beverages
>> Exercise 3 to 5 times

Weighing the Numbers – An Example
A person weighing 175 pounds, who weight trains for 45 minutes and runs at 5 mph for 30 minutes, will burn approximately 500 calories in a single exercise session. That same person can get the same result by simply choosing to get a sugar-free venti iced green tea versus the same size Mocha Frappuccino at Starbucks after work (500 calories)!

Keep the following in mind when it comes to your food choices throughout the day:
>> Get the right nutrients for good health from fruits, vegetables, grains, dairy, proteins and essential fats.
>> When shopping for groceries stay away from the middle aisles. All food located on the perimeter of the store are your healthiest (and freshest) options.
>> Exercise portion control (regardless of what is on your plate).
>> Eat slowly. Most people eat faster then they digest which results in overeating.
>> Stay within your daily caloric intake (especially if you are looking to maintain or lose weight).
>> Be conscious of making healthy choices more often throughout the day to ensure that the hard work that you put into your workouts in the gym produce the overall results you are looking to achieve.

If you're looking at getting started TODAY ... check out the ACTIV Personal Training "Heart Healthy" workshop being offered AT NO COST on Saturday, February 14th! Visit us at www.activ-pt.com for more information.

70%
OF YOUR RESULTS WILL COME FROM WHAT YOU EAT

30%
OF YOUR RESULTS WILL COME FROM WHAT YOU DO

Figure S2-4: "Heart Healthy Workshop" Facebook Post

Although Facebook is useful, it doesn't guarantee that everyone who likes your page will see every post. If you happen to have clients as "friends" on Facebook, you can "share" this post in a private message. This will provide a higher percentage of readers for any post on your page.

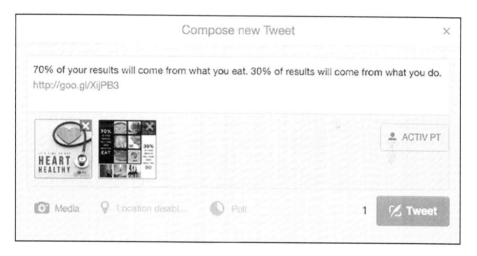

Figure S2-5: "Heart Healthy Workshop" Tweets

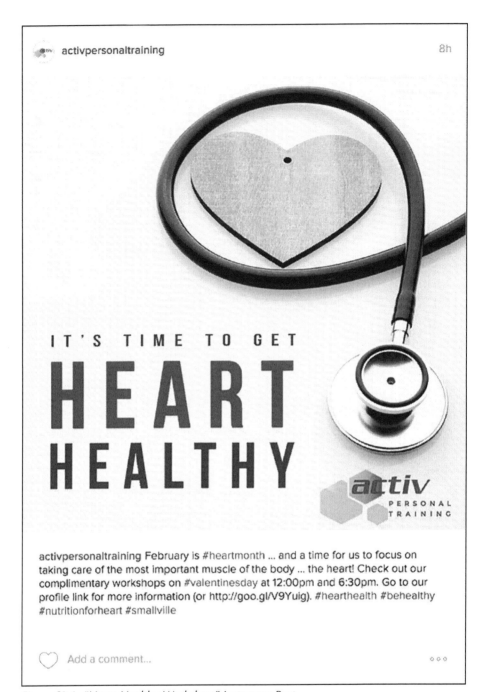

Figure S2-6: "Heart Healthy Workshop" Instagram Post

Figure S2-7: ACTIV Personal Training Promotional Gear (S2)

You, your staff (if you have other trainers working for you) and your clients are your best marketing and advertising. Wear your logo with pride and reward others for their hard work and dedication with unique gear!

Be sure to choose apparel and accessories that match the quality and integrity of your business. If you are providing services at a higher price point than your competitors, ensure the same quality is consistent in anything tangible that represents your business (i.e., business cards, handouts, t-shirts, hats, etc.). If you charge a high price for training but use sub-par materials, the inconsistency is evident to your audience.

attendees of the event. The business owner may also be willing to provide the location at no cost (because you are bringing potential customers into their establishment).

Marketing Checklist

1. Produce one page handouts and/or signage. ☐
2. Produce landing page (or blog post) on website. ☐
3. Get marketing and promotional materials printed. ☐
4. Send out email to current client database. ☐
5. Start grassroots marketing initiatives. ☐
6. Produce a minimum of five (5) Facebook posts to promote during the advertising period. ☐
7. Produce a minimum of ten (10) Tweets to promote during the advertising period. ☐
8. Send reminder email to current client database one week prior to program start date. ☐
9. Evaluate the marketing strategy. ☐

SAMPLE #3

TRAINING & CONDITIONING FOR GOLFERS

activ PERSONAL TRAINING

GOLFERS

March, the first official month of spring, marks a time of renewal and preparation for the summer months. It also marks the start of the golfing season (or at least the time where people are starting to get ready to get on the links)! This marketing strategy is designed to promote a small group training program for golfers looking to improve their golf game over the summer months.

Target Audience

The target audience includes people living within 20 miles of the ACTIV Personal Training location, who are over the age of 14 years, are avid golfers, and are looking for effective solutions to help them achieve their goals of more consistent play.

Marketing Message

Summer is just around the corner and are YOU ready to shed your winter layers and reveal your six pack abs? Let ACTIV Personal Training help you get ready for the summer with the "Spring Shape Up" program!

With over 15 years of experience, helping people transform their lives, ACTIV Personal Training has partnered with people of all ages and abilities in an effort to help them achieve their goals through exercise and nutrition. Our proprietary programs include scientifically proven methods and strategies to help people improve strength, power, flexibility, balance, core stability and endurance to produce more consistent results in their golf game.

Duration of the Program
- 12 weeks (April 1 to September 30)

Services Provided
- 10 x Access to "Training & Conditioning for Golfers" classes

between April 1st and September 30th. Classes are offered:

- Tuesdays   12:00pm to 1:00pm & 6:30pm to 7:30pm
- Thursdays   12:00pm to 1:00pm & 6:30pm to 7:30pm
- Saturdays   10:00am to 11:00am

- Additional 10 Class Passes can be purchased at any time during the program
- $50 GIFT CERTIFICATE: Redeemable at Golf Town (expires September 30, 2016)

Promotional Material(s)
1. One page flyer (8.5" x 11")
2. Email template (current clients and opt-in database)
3. Landing page or blog post (www.activ-pt.com)
4. Social media communications (Facebook, Twitter and Instagram)
5. ACTIV Personal Training t-shirt and gear (giveaways)

One Page Flyer
The one-page flyer (8.5" x 11") should include the following:
1. Company logo
2. Contact information (address, phone number, website, and email address)
3. Workshop name, details and benefits to attendees
4. Deadline for sign up (i.e., RSVP to trainer@activ-pt.com)
5. Call to action (i.e., "Limited Spots Available")

Landing Page or Blog Post
The website should include a promotional landing page and/or blog post providing information about the complimentary "Heart Healthy" workshops and should include the following:
1. Workshop name, details and benefits to attendees
2. Link to download One Page Flyer (8.5" x 11")
3. Link to Shopping Cart to purchase personal training sessions (using Discount Code)
4. Image of ACTIV Personal Training t-shirt and gear (optional)
5. Call to action (i.e., "Click HERE to secure your spot today!")

Grassroots Marketing Strategies
1. Key Influencer(s)

Identify at least five (5) businesses in your local area who have clients who would benefit from the "Training & Conditioning for Golfers" program. Examples include:

- Local medical professionals who frequently see golfers experiencing pain or discomfort (i.e., chiropractors, massage therapists, nutritionists)
- Schools or academies for golf (i.e., offering training programs and one-on-one lessons)
- Sporting goods stores or Golf Pro Shops (at golf courses)
- Local retailers and business owners who also have a love of golf

Reach out and provide them with information about your program. If they are interested in promoting the program at their place of business (i.e., putting up posters, handing out information) you can return the favor by offering to promote their business to your current client list (i.e., a blog post, inclusion in your next eNewsletter, mention in an upcoming broadcast email, etc.).

2. Promotional Products (Giveaways)
As a part of the 12 week program, all participants receive a $50 Gift Certificate at Green Hills Golf Club (which can be used in the Pro Shop). They must purchase a minimum of $10 Class Passes ($175.00 value) to receive the gift certificate. A limit of one gift certificate is provided per participant.

Marketing Checklist
1. Produce one page handouts and/or signage. ☐
2. Produce landing page (or blog post) on website. ☐
3. Get marketing and promotional materials printed. ☐
4. Send out email to current client database. ☐
5. Start grassroots marketing initiatives. ☐
6. Produce a minimum of five (5) Facebook posts to promote during the advertising period. ☐
7. Produce a minimum of ten (10) Tweets to promote during the advertising period. ☐
8. Send reminder email to client database (one week prior) ☐
9. Evaluate the marketing strategy. ☐

TRAINING & CONDITIONING FOR
GOLFERS

DOESN'T IT FEEL GOOD TO HIT A "NICE SHOT"?

It's the moment you hit the perfect ball, with the effortless swing, straight path and crisp sound, that makes you fall in love all over again. Unfortunately, for most golfers, this experience is few and far between. The consistency that is required to produce the perfect swing every time, regardless of the situation, demands more than just athletic ability ... it requires golf-specific:

- Strength
- Power
- Flexibility
- Balance,
- Core stability
- Body awareness
- Endurance

Although Pro Shops are filled with various gadgets and gimmicks for increasing accuracy and shot distance, the world's best golfers know that consistent results comes from a carefully tailored fitness program.

In preparation for the busy golf season, ACTIV Personal Training is offering "Training and Conditioning for Golfers" from April 5th to September 29th. These small group training sessions are offered on:

- Tuesdays   12:00pm to 1:00pm & 6:30pm to 7:30pm
- Thursdays   12:00pm to 1:00pm & 6:30pm to 7:30pm
- Saturdays   10:00am to 11:00am

To register for the program you must purchase a 10 Class Pass ($175.00). Participants can attend any of the classes offered, on a "first come, first serve" basis. Once all classes on the pass are used up, an additional 10 Class Passes can be purchased.

SIGN UP FOR "TRAINING AND CONDITIONING FOR GOLF" AND RECEIVE A $50 GIFT CERTIFICATE FROM GREEN HILLS GOLF CLUB!

activ PERSONAL TRAINING

FOR MORE INFORMATION VISIT

www.activ-pt.com

ACTIV Personal Training
123 Anywhere Street
Smallville, CA 12345
P: (123) 456-7890

Figure S3-1: "Training & Conditioning for Golfers" Handout

CREATIVE
MARKETING
IDEA

Be sure to print at least 500 sheets (8.5" x 11") to hand out during your campaign:

- To current clients
- For clients to share with friends/family members
- At speaking events or workshops
- At partner locations (businesses that you promote and vice versa)

ABOUT US   SERVICES   PROGRAMS   RESOURCES   CONTACT

TRAINING & CONDITIONING FOR GOLFERS

March 11, 2016 By: Andrea Oh - 3 Comments

LIKE IT? SHARE IT!

DOESN'T IT FEEL GOOD TO HIT A "NICE SHOT"?
It's the moment you hit the perfect ball, with the effortless swing, straight path and crisp sound, that makes you fall in love all over again. Unfortunately, for most golfers, this experience is few and far between. The consistency that is required to produce the perfect swing every time, regardless of the situation, demands more than just athletic ability ... it requires golf-specific:

- Strength
- Power
- Flexibility
- Balance,
- Core stability
- Body awareness
- Endurance

Although Pro Shops are filled with various gadgets and gimmicks for increasing accuracy and shot distance, the world's best golfers know that consistent results comes from a carefully tailored fitness program.

In preparation for the busy golf season, ACTIV Personal Training is offering "Training and Conditioning for Golfers" from April 5th to September 29th. These small group training sessions are offered on:

- Tuesdays   12:00pm to 1:00pm & 6:30pm to 7:30pm
- Thursdays   12:00pm to 1:00pm & 6:30pm to 7:30pm
- Saturdays   10:00am to 11:00am

To register for the program you must purchase a 10 Class Pass ($175.00). Participants can attend any of the classes offered, on a "first come, first serve" basis. Once all classes on the pass are used up, an additional 10 Class Passes can be purchased.

SIGN UP FOR "TRAINING AND CONDITIONING FOR GOLF" AND RECEIVE A $50 GIFT CERTIFICATE FROM GREEN HILLS GOLF CLUB!

CLICK HERE TO DOWNLOAD THE BROCHURE OR EMAIL US TODAY!

Figure S3-2: "Training & Conditioning for Golfers" Landing Page (www.activ-pt.com)

Be sure to post the URL to this page on all of your social media networks (at least once a week):

- Facebook (personal page)
- Facebook (business page)
- Twitter
- Instagram (unique image to promote this page)
- Google+

| Send | Reply | Quote | Responses | Attach | Signatures | Save | Sidebar |

Andrea Oh <trainer@activ-pt.com> ∨

To:

Cc:

Bcc:

Reply-To:

Subject: Doesn't it feel good to hit a "nice shot"?

Variable Width ∨ | A↓ A↑ | ■ a | B *I* U̲ | ≣ ≣ ≣∨ | ∞ </> Ɪ

<NAME>,

It's no secret that I love the game of golf. I think about it all year long and train specifically to improve my own game. Well ... now I'm offering "Training and Conditioning for Golfers" to let others benefit from a focused program, too!

Starting on April 5th (and going until September 29th), ACTIV Personal Training will be offering golf-specific, small group personal training sessions You already know how much I personally enjoy the game and now I'm bringing this passion and knowledge to all of you!

These small group training sessions are offered on:
- Tuesdays   12:00pm to 1:00pm & 6:30pm to 7:30pm
- Thursdays   12:00pm to 1:00pm & 6:30pm to 7:30pm
- Saturdays   10:00am to 11:00am

To be a part of the program you need to purchase at least a 10 Class Pass ($175.00). Participants can attend any of the classes offered, on a "first come, first serve" basis. Once all classes on the pass are used up, additional 10 Class Passes can be purchased (there are over 60 classes offered over the season). In addition, participant will receive a $50 Gift Certificate to the Green Hills Golf Club!

If you are interested in attending this workshop, please give me a call at (123) 456-7890 or email me at trainer@activ-pt.com.

Also, if you or someone you know might be interested in joining the "Training & Conditioning for Golfers" sessions, please have them contact me or have them visit the website at www.activ-pt.com for details.

Thank you again for your ongoing support and commitment to your health and fitness.

Have a GREAT day!

Andrea.

ANDREA OH
Owner & Head Strength and Conditioning Coach

Figure S3-3: "Training & Conditioning for Golfers" Email to Clients

As a follow up to this email, assuming clients that are not currently training with you will receive this, give each recipient on this list a phone call. You can easily reference this email as the basis of your call, cultivate a meaningful conversation, and help identify whether (or not) this program is ideal for this particular client.

156

ACTIV Personal Training
March 13, 2016 at 8:41am

FITNESS TIP OF THE DAY:
Learn from the obstacles and challenges you face as you work to becoming a better golfer (and athlete).

Working towards any goal, big or small, will include obstacles that get in the way of your overall success. You will face:
- Better golfers
- Missed shots
- Bad club choices and anxious moments
- Thoughts of "giving up" or "quitting"
- Setbacks (i.e., injuries, sickness, unexpected travel)

Regardless of the situation, find a way to dig deep, believe in yourself, and find the courage from within to overcome the obstacles ahead of you.

Some of the most successful people in the world face significant challenges, that could have ended their careers if they didn't overcome their fears and doubt. Here are a few examples to put things into perspective:

MICHAEL JORDAN
"I've missed more than 9000 shots in my career. I've lost almost 300 games. 26 times I've been trusted to take the game winning shot ... and missed. I've failed over and over and over again in my life. And that is why I succeed."

SYLVESTER STALLONE (aka. Rocky Balboa)
His script for "Rocky" was rejected repeatedly before it was accepted (at one point he had to sell his dog to make ends meet). In 1976, the movie won Oscars for Best Picture, Best Director, and Best Actor.

MIA HAMM
Mia was born with a partial clubfoot but overcame her physical challenges to become one of the greatest female soccer players in the world.

The ability to face adversity and overcome challenges is the difference between failure and success. Take a moment to think of where YOU find the strength to pick yourself up, dust yourself off and keep going.

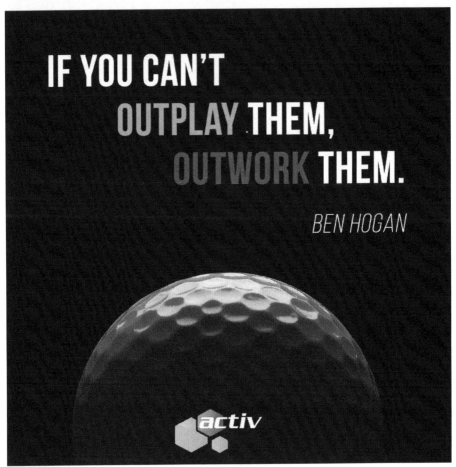

Figure S3-4: "Training & Conditioning for Golfers" Facebook Post

Although Facebook is useful, it doesn't guarantee that everyone who likes your page will see every post. If you happen to have clients as "friends" on Facebook, you can "share" this post in a private message. This will provide a higher percentage of readers for any post on your page.

Figure S3-5: "Training & Conditioning for Golfers" Tweets

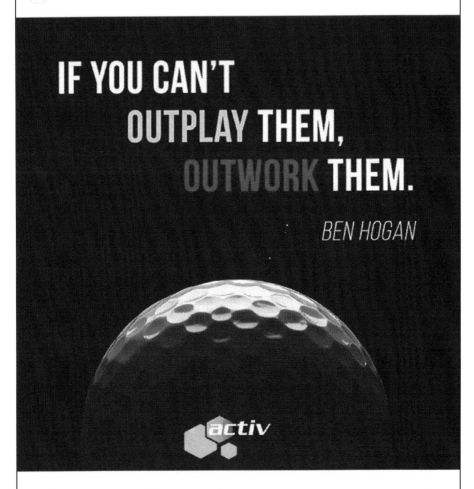

IF YOU CAN'T
OUTPLAY THEM,
OUTWORK THEM.

BEN HOGAN

activpersonaltraining Note to self ... "If you can't outplay them, outwork them." Join us for our "Training & Conditioning for Golfers" sessions starting on April 5th (running until September 29th). For more formation visit www.activ-pt.com! #golffitness #teetime #activepersonaltraining #smallville

Add a comment...

Figure S3-6: "Training & Conditioning for Golfers" Instagram Post

Figure S3-7: ACTIV Personal Training Gift Certificate (with co-promotion)

This co-promotional gift certificate can be used as a marketing tool for both you and the partnered business. You can give this coupon to all participants that sign up for the program and the partner can advertise this program to loyal customers at their store who would want the $50 Gift Certificate. It's a "win-win" situation for both businesses!

Chapter 17:
Final Thoughts

Since the release of "The Business of Personal Training: Essential Guide for the Successful Personal Trainer", the global economy has drastically changed. The power of the Internet (in this ever changing world) may have you wondering if owning your own personal training business is a good long term plan.

Here are the facts ...

We live in a world driven by technology and convenience. The world's largest and most established companies are closing their doors because consumers have found easier and more convenient ways to get what they need. For example:

- Retailers are closing their doors because Amazon.com and Zappos.com are selling the same products at lower prices (and shipping them right to people's homes).
- Radio stations are being replaced by smartphones and Sirius XM
- Television stations are being replaced by Netflix, Hulu and Shomi
- Newspapers are being replaced by the Internet
- Magazines are being replaced by mobile apps (i.e., Newsstand and Next Issue)
- Books are being replaced by ebooks on Kindle and Kobo

Consumers are no longer required to leave the comfort of their homes to learn, work, be entertained or even get groceries. Everything can be conveniently accessed online.

Should you be worried that the Internet will also take the place of personal trainers and fitness professionals ... like you?

NOT IN OUR LIFETIME!

In a world where people want quick solutions to problems ... improving one's fitness and health can't be rushed. In fact, in a society where we are all becoming more sedentary, our profession is needed more than ever! The Internet has yet to figure out how to keep someone motivated and focused on a long term goal without the knowledge, expertise and human interaction provided by one-on-one personal training.

People rarely rush experiences or interactions with the people they respect, appreciate and enjoy spending time with ... which is the goal of every personal training relationship. For example, you wouldn't rush a meal at your favourite restaurant if the food is delicious and the service is impeccable. You also wouldn't rush a performance by your favorite musical artist when the music has you singing at the top of your lungs and dancing up a storm.

In a more "automated world", people are craving real human interactions, unique experiences and a personal touch. This is why the service industry (i.e., businesses that create unique experiences for their customers) won't be affected by this technological shift. Personal trainers can only benefit if they continue to deliver exceptional service and heartfelt support!

In fact, over the last ten years I've worked with a handful of companies that have attempted virtual personal training (or online personal training services) ... and none of them have proven to be successful.

So ... breathe a sigh of relief and leverage the benefits technology can provide in marketing and strategically growing your business!

My parting thoughts still remain the same (as the previous book) ... but may provide new insight after reading the contents of this book.

Love what you do.

If you love what you do, it rarely feels like work. It becomes a labor of love that is exciting, challenging, fun and filled with unique experiences that make for wonderful memories. Embracing a career that you love takes effort, but is definitely worth it.

Be curious.

Experience the world with all of your senses. What you see, hear, smell, taste and touch may provide the spark of inspiration that becomes the next great "thing" for your business. Great ideas come from the most common experiences. Many people ponder on ideas but entrepreneurs take those ideas and act on them. Entrepreneurs make things happen!

Find your own market niche.

Develop a special competency in fitness and health that differentiates you from everyone else. Don't be afraid to be creative and look for needs in the market that other personal trainers may not have considered. Great entrepreneurs provide products and services that are better or different than what everyone else is doing.

Think globally, act locally.

As intimidating as this sounds, achieving "world-class" expertise may not be as difficult as you might think. If you pick an area of specialization, focus on it, and learn as much as you can from leading experts. In no time you can accumulate in depth knowledge and skills that can significantly benefit your business. While you can never become the world authority on everything, you can definitely become a world authority on one thing.

Learn from the best.

When you think about personal training, fitness, exercise, and various specialty areas in the field, ask yourself:
- "Who do I aspire to be like in 5 or 10 years?"
- "Currently, who are the world's leading experts in the field?"

Try to learn from these people (i.e. what they know, what they do in business, where they speak/present). You may be surprised how quickly you learn from them. Over time you may become "that" person to another personal trainer.

Do your homework.
There are so many resources available to learn about fitness, exercise, nutrition, and business (in general). Dedicate time each day to gathering valuable information that will help you:
- Become a better personal trainer.
- Become a better business owner.
- Become a better marketer.
- Become a better sales person.

Mentors may be one of the best resources to draw upon for information, but be sure to respect their busy schedules and responsibilities to their own business.

Evolve your brand.
Continue to fine tune your unique personal brand (including your mission, vision and core values). Your clients will respect you more if you are genuine and effectively communicate your brand proposition as a way to accommodate their needs. Celebrate your strengths and recognize your weaknesses in an effort to better match your service offering to the right clients.

Do the work.
Some people may just get lucky and become incredibly successful without having to work very hard. For the 99 percent of us that live in the real world, this is not the case. Successful entrepreneurs (and successful people) generally work very hard (and in a smart way). What others may perceive as "luck" is merely the action they choose to take when an opportunity comes their way.

This is the second book in the "Business of Personal Training" series. For more information on upcoming topics and release dates, go to www. BUSINESS.fit.

TESTIMONIALS

I've had the opportunity to work with Andrea over the past couple of years while consulting on two fitness-related projects, one a sports club and the other a fitness equipment remanufacturing company. With over 40 years of experience in various areas of the fitness industry it is always refreshing to come across someone as unique and talented as Ms. Oh!

She is truly "lightening in a bottle" and approaches her work with laser focus and purpose. Andrea is always very present when collaborating and can really add value to any meeting. In fact I've been taken to school more than a few times when it comes to her command of fitness training, marketing, branding and social media.

Most importantly, Andrea possesses great poise when communicating with others and seems to always be the head of her class in any group setting. Team building is essential in the fitness business and Andrea exemplifies this at a very high level. In contrast, she knows when to take the lead and when to take a back seat in an effort to ensure a group gets the job done in an effective manner. She knows how to "play nice in the sandbox with others."

Don't get me wrong, she may be an expert in the business of personal training, sales and marketing, but her fitness background is perhaps her greatest strength. Having been both an elite athlete and highly certified teacher it is a wonder to me why she didn't write this book sooner!

Buyer be warned: You are in very good hands!

Gary Mirsky
President, ProClub Management Group
www.proclubgroup.com

We couldn't imagine where our company would be today without Andrea! Since joining Swank Media, she has lit up our professional (and personal) lives with her positivity, innovative thinking, and ability to find solutions to the most challenging problems. She has been an inspiration to our business by contributing her knowledge, experience and expertise in various industries.

Although she is recognized as an expert in the fitness industry, her talents go much further. She has a passion for business development and marketing strategy, is a focused project manager and leader, a talented copywriter and editor, and so much more! Not only does she have an extremely wide spectrum of talents her ability to see projects through and her determination for the team has made her a key leader in our business.

We've never met anyone so hard working and humble in all our years of business and can't honestly say enough good things about her. I would recommend her time and time again as she has seriously changed our lives for the better. I look forward to the future, growing alongside her and continuing to learn from her.

Manuel Tomašir & Marta Tomašir
Founding Partners, Swank Media Inc.
www.swankmedia.ca

Andrea has proved herself to be an accretive addition to the Soul Studios team. Her tenacity to get things done, questioning of the norm and push for continuous improvement have been refreshing and has allowed the company to improve the overall customer experience. Andrea's previous experience and expertise in marketing and strategy have identified areas of improvement where proven solutions can be suggested and applied. Andrea has a keen ability to see things from the customer perspective which has allowed for execution of initiatives we may not have understood otherwise. We believe the changes implemented so far will improve the company and look forward to completing many more.

Jamie Davis, Cathy Sinclair-Smith & Steve Smith
Owners, Soul Hot Yoga & Soul Spin Studio
www.soulstudios.ca

I have had the pleasure of working with Andrea for several years. She has been a site partner, colleague (and confidante) with Today's Growth Consultant and Income Store. It has been exciting to watch her grow as a digital branding and marketing leader as she has brought new ideas and effective processes to our operations, making our company even better. She has an incredible capacity for thinking "big" yet doing what is necessary to turn big ideas into reality. Her focused drive, ambition and creativity have been instrumental in building her authority sites, the virtual real estate of our site partners, and our company as a whole. Andrea is an innovator, a leader and a woman that gets the job done ... RIGHT.

In addition, she has a way of bringing people together, fostering teamwork and helping others rise to the occasion. This is one of the many traits that makes her a great leader and project manager. We have clients from a wide variety of industries, but only a handful that change our company and how we operate for the better. I am blessed to know her, work with her, and have her guidance.

Allen Wilterdink
COO, Today's Growth Consultant & Income Store
(www.incomestore.com)